# STEVE DIGGLE'S ROCK & ROLL ODYSSEY
# HARMONY IN MY HEAD

## TERRY RAWLINGS
### INTRODUCTION BY MICK JONES

Helter Skelter Publishing

# STEVE DIGGLE'S ROCK & ROLL ODYSSEY
# HARMONY IN MY HEAD

## TERRY RAWLINGS
### INTRODUCTION BY MICK JONES

ODEON HAMMERSMITH Tel. 01-748-4081
Manager: Philip Leivers
STRAIGHT MUSIC presents
BUZZCOCKS
EVENING 7-30 p.m.
Saturday, Nov. 4th, 1978
STALLS
£2·50
BLOCK
22
/ B30

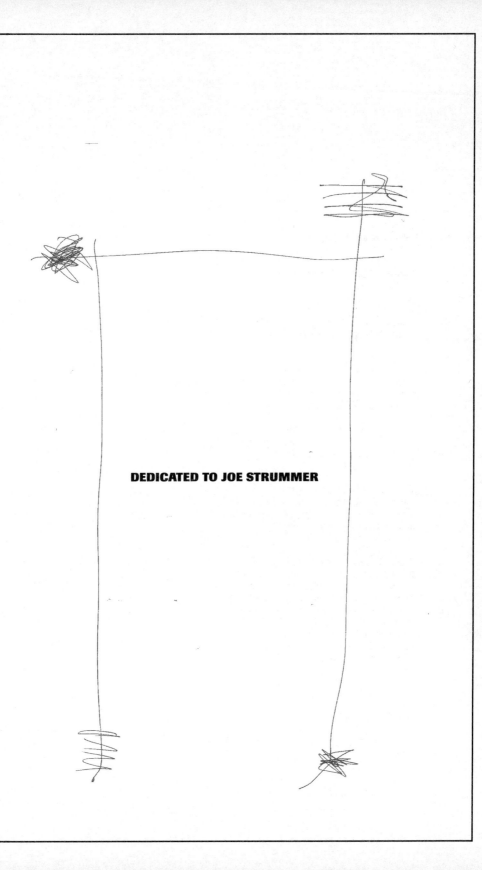

**DEDICATED TO JOE STRUMMER**

This edition published in 2003 by
**Helter Skelter Publishing**
4 Denmark Street, London WC2H 8LL.

Design by Terry Rawlings and Paul McEvoy.
Additional design, layout and artwork by
Chris Wilson @ CWDGA.

Printed in Great Britain by The Bath Press.

A CIP record for this book is available from
the British Library.

**1-900924-37-4**

## ACKNOWLEDGEMENTS & THANKS

Sean & Michael at Helter Skelter ... thanks for your patience.

Mick Jones, Glen Matlock, Mani Mounfield and Alan McGee
for contributions.

Eon Ballinger (plain old Ian to us) for early inspiration,
Paul McEvoy and all @ Bold for the usual creative doings,
Diane Daly for sanctuary and her laptop, Terry (the badge) Bunton,
Andrew McNellis for back cover shot, Welsh Pete for background,
'Rock' Pete, Bob Morris for bits'n'bobs... Clwyd Parry being
one of them, Cherry Red for pix, Lesley Benson and Dawn, Jim Guynan,
Jim McDonald, Gary Crowley, Holly Cara Price and all @ Renegade
Nation, Big Tim Farazmand, Rob Harvey and Josh Goode for the
champagne and enthusiasm, Stuart Batsford for trying,
Stephanie Bennett @ Delilah, all the photographers who have
contributed to Steve's shockingly limited archive (definitely not a
hoarder) and anyone else we may have inadvertently omitted.

Special thanks to Little Steven Van Zandt and his Underground Garage.

## STEVE DIGGLE AND TERRY RAWLINGS 2003

# CONTENTS

## INTRODUCTION

I first met Steve Diggle outside the Screen On The Green, Islington, in late August '76. We were exhausted from watching The Outlaw Josey Wales three times in a row. The show didn't start 'til midnight, Sunday night - Sex Pistols, The Clash and The Buzzcocks - all for £1 with refreshments available.
When the picture finished, we built the stage. We had all heard about this outfit from Manchester, and we were all keen to check them out first hand. They were great and it was the start of an association that has lasted more than 25 years.
On the Anarchy tour, Dec '76, my first time in Manchester, at the Electric Circus ... The Buzzcocks seemed to me to represent the whole new thing in that city.

Early the next year, 1977, we invited Steve and the boys down for a return engagement - it was The Clash, The Buzzcocks, The Slits and The Subway Sect - plus all night uncensored Kung Fu films at this place called the Coliseum, Harlesden. Due to the cost of living it was now £1.50 to get in. Steve and I became firm friends from the off and have remained so ever since.
Like minds I guess - fellow journeymen and all that...

Love, inspiration and rock&roll.

Mick
xx

## MICK JONES 2003

## FOREWORDS

Steve Diggle I first saw live in 1977. The Buzzcocks changed
my life with Orgasm Addict and What do I Get. The first LP
Another Music In A Different Kitchen was one of the
greatest LP's punk ever produced. It led to Joy Division.
I saw them about 20 times. Me and Primal Scream loved
them and travelled all over Scotland to see them.
Diggle became a really good songwriter as well with
Why She's A Girl From The Chainstore. In 1993 I was in LA
with the Scream trying to finish the follow up album to
Screamadelica. We all got roaring drunk and went to see
them play - now with Tony and Phil on board - to our
astonishment they were still great. Kurt Cobain, I knew
through mutual friends, also thought they were classic.
Diggle to me is the spirit, the never-say-die attitude
of The Buzzcocks. He is as important to me as Mick Jones
is to me in The Clash. Diggle always meant it. In a world
of reality television it's important to me that people like that
are still there to remind me how mediocre the culture
of Britain has become. Diggle is a hero to me and
thousands of others from that era and The Buzzcocks are
iconic heroes to the day I die. Long live the Diggle!!

**ALAN MCGEE 2003**

I've known Steve for over 25 years, and he's a boozin' shagger, and I love him dearly...

**GLEN MATLOCK 2003**

I first went to see the Buzzcocks in nineteen seventy-eight in Oldham. I was wearing a Loreto Collage blazer.
After the gig I went back stage to meet Steve and shake his hand. Somehow his cigarette caught my sleeve and my jacket started to go up in flames. Steve said "Eh mate your jacket's on fire". I said, "I know it's a blazer."
They're a top band! I also remember the King's Hall with "The Fall" supporting (Bingo Masters breakout).
What do I get?
No love, what do I get?
No sleep at night, what do I get?
Nothing that's nice, what do I get?
Nothing at all at all at all,
cos I don't get yooooooooou!

**MANI MOUNFIELD 2003**

# CHAPTER ONE
# GRIM UP NORTH

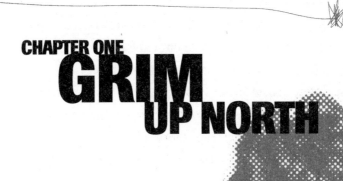

ODEON HAMMERSMITH Tel. 01-748-4081
Manager: Philip Leivers
STRAIGHT MUSIC presents
BUZZCOCKS

EVENING 7-30 p.m.
Saturday, Nov. 4th, 1978

STALLS
£2·50

BLOCK

22

R30

I was born to Janet and Eric Diggle on the 7th of May 1955, the year of Rock'n'Roll, in Mosside Manchester. I was the oldest of four children, the others being my brother Philip and two sisters Wendy and Sandra. We all got off to a relatively good start living in a nice house with a garden not far from the family business, a kids' clothes shop on the Stockport Road. My dad had his own car in his twenties, a Flying Standard, which looked like an American police car. We were all healthy and happy. Of course, it didn't last because my dad gave out too much credit and the shop closed down when nobody came back to settle up.

We then had to move to an old terrace house with a back yard in Dewar Street, which was in a rundown part of Manchester called Bradford. Bradford looked exactly like those old black-and-white episodes of Coronation Street only a lot worse - it was drab and dirty with rows and rows of cramped red brick houses all connected to one and other by washing lines. Each house backed on to an alleyway and each street had its own gang of teddy boys and street urchins. They would hang about on the corners and beat the shit out of each other every week.

Now, before I go on, am I right in thinking that people normally skip this part of anybody's autobiography? Let's face it, aren't most people's childhood experiences on the whole pretty much the same? Of course, that's unless you were brought up in some pretty dire circumstances and forced up chimneys or down a mine. As I wasn't, I'll try to be as brief as possible so we can get down to the sex, drugs and rock'n'roll. Conveniently enough, my earliest musical memory is also my earliest sexual one albeit in a very innocent way. I nonetheless managed to combine the two. It was 1962. I had a friend called Ian James that lived across the road from me who had an older sister called Linda, and it was thanks to her that I discovered both. This was at a time when people like Charlie Drake and Rolf Harris ruled the world and music was very much a novelty, songs like 'My Boomerang Won't Come Back', 'Two Little Boys' and 'Three Wheels On My Wagon'. There was a radio program called Children's Favorites that played that shit all the time, but not Linda. Oh no. She had the first Beatles album Please Please Me and the first Dylan one. She had actual albums, which seemed like such a big deal. She also had an old Dansette record player which had loads of Beatle bubble gum cards stuck on the inside of the lid. Linda would play those records while drying her long blonde hair in front of the mirror, using a huge pink hair dryer, which looked like a Russian Sputnik. I remember thinking that this was the most sophisticated thing I had ever seen. Up until then I thought everyone dried his or her hair with a towel like me. Now for a very impressionable seven-year-old you can imagine that this was really something else! But that wasn't all! Linda also had a guitar - it was only one of those cheap little Spanish acoustics but it was still an actual guitar. It was on one of those memorable hair-drying occasions that I first picked up a guitar: the Beatles were playing in the background and I plucked a string.

That note resounded right though my body watching Linda with her Morphy Richards and listening to 'Twist And Shout'; now that felt like my first sexual experience plus it introduced me to rock'n'roll.

After that I became obsessed with music and the Beatles. My cousin Alan Castle who lived a couple of streets away was a teddy boy and he was always blasting out Little Richard and Chuck Berry which is fine but, after discovering the Fabs, liking Elvis seemed a bit out of date. I got my Mum to buy me a black turtleneck jumper and I combed my hair forward.

I think I knew what I wanted to do with my life from very early on and it wasn't going to involve working, In fact, I was and still am a dedicated conscientious objector to all aspects of it.

The Beatles had shown me the way to go and I wasn't going to be talked out of it. After all, as they were all working class lads, and came from up north, surely anyone could do it.

However I still had primary school to finish. To my knowledge, Bradford Memorial wasn't famous for nurturing child stars. That's not to say it didn't have its moments, well it had a moment. One of the Swinging Blue Jeans had a daughter that went there. I didn't know his name, but he was the one that thought he was John Lennon. I can't remember her name either – "Little Blue Jeans". Anyway, Big Blue Jeans turned up one day to pick her up. 'Hippy Hippy Shake' was in the charts so he was making the most of it. He actually had the band outfit on, the light colored jeans and leather waistcoat. I'm sure he even had a sun tan. I was mesmerized, "Fucking hell a pop star, and he really looks like a pop star, too." It was all very exotic and exciting with all the kids surrounding him while he signed a few autographs. It wasn't exactly Blue Jean mania as he drove off but it left another lasting impression.

After Bradford Memorial (which for some bizarre reason was in Manchester and not in Bradford), I went to the impressive-sounding (deceptively) Higher Openshaw High, Monkee Davy Jones' old school. All the new kids were gathered together on our first day in order to meet the headmaster who was going to welcome us to the place. He was obviously very proud of his school's two famous pupils, the other one being Rifleman John Beckley a soldier who had been awarded a Victoria Cross for shooting Germans. He gave us this really long speech about how Davy Jones and Beckley had been such good students and how they'd gone on to achieve great things, meaning we could all do the same. I remember thinking, 'Wow! Davy fucking Jones went here! He's on me Tele at five and he lives in Hollywood: how's he done that? This man's obviously talking bollocks.' He then held up a toilet seat and a bathroom tap that had been ripped off in acts of vandalism. Years later I found out Davy had gone there and I thought maybe I should go back and sort of say something to the kids like "Look, kids, your old head was right. You can achieve things. See me? I'm in a punk rock band called the Buzzcocks". That would have been the order: Beckley, Jones, and Diggle. Then I found out Davy never went back so I thought fuck 'em.

I only stayed at Openshaw for about a year before we were on the move again, this time to a place called Mosston and the Hulme housing estate. This was a horrible backwater shithole that was built for the miners' families after all their nice terraced houses had been pulled down in the name of progress. It was being heralded as new architecture at the time but of course we now know it simply as tower blocks. Basically generations of miners and their families were taken out of rows of houses where they had lived happily side by side forever and stacked up on top of one another. 'No Ball Games' signs were everywhere and, of course, any sense of community was destroyed. How's that for a bizarre concept? By day, you're sent down a hole in a lift hundreds of feet below the earth and then when you get home you're hoisted hundreds of feet in the air? Those estates were quickly run down in the way all those tower blocks were dirty filthy lifts and stairwells and underground car parks that became famous for prostitutes, but Hey! That's progress. I ended up at another school called Wright Robinson High. My first day there was a completely different experience from Openshaw: here, I was met at the gates by the school's welcome committee, a gang of skinheads who reliably informed me I was going to have my head shoved down the toilet at breaktime.

The whole area had an air of underlying doom and violence about it, which was best exemplified when a mate of mine, George Ashcroft, had his head blown off with a twelve-bore shotgun by another mate of mine Alan Beswick. That wasn't your average kid's accident. Apparently, it was his dad's gun that was just left lying about and nobody realized it was loaded. What does that tell you? It was eventually put down to accidental death – so no harm done there then! That certainly left a bit of a cloud over the estate. Despite these minor setbacks, I actually got down to learning a fair bit during my teenage years at Robinson. In retrospect, it wasn't too bad a place.

It certainly had its perks, mainly due to it being a mixed school, meaning that opportunities for a bit of adolescent fumbling were greatly increased.

That big day finally arrived when I was around sixteen and by now a reasonably presentable mod.

Doctor Martens were a new number then. I wore the shoe version with a check Ben Sherman shirt and this great navy blue rain Mac. Thinking back, it was more of an early Suedehead look than Mod. The music was the same: all Soul, Jackie Wilson and the Bar Kays I remember were the big things at the time. I bought a Lambretta TV 175 on hire purchase, which cost me exactly one hundred and seventy five quid. Simple maths, that. It was red and cream with the engine bored out and fitted with a lightweight-racing piston to make it a 200. I never changed the badge so nobody knew the difference. It was the most liberating thing I ever did, it opened up a whole New World. I was independently mobile for the first time.

My best mate Geoff Hyde had a Vespa GP 200 and we would meet up in the centre of Manchester with other mods and cruise around about twenty-handed, getting accused of terrorizing the place just by riding through it. Girls, however, would absolutely love it, which brings me back to the point. I'll call her 'Eleanor Rigby' to safeguard her ignominy – for reasons that will become clear shortly. Anyway, I was seeing this girl who was your archetypal Sixties doll bird: long straight black hair, all eyelashes, and miniskirt. Fantastic! The trouble was when it came to the crunch, I had nowhere to take her, nowhere private anyway. So I opted for the quietest place I could think of, the local graveyard.

I scooted around in the mist with her on the back until I found a suitable plot; you know the sort, low level not too springy, and bang! We lost it there and then. I can't remember if she was too happy about the location or, for that matter, the performance. I just wish I could remember the name on the headstone. Fucking Goth or what? Tell that to Marilyn Manson. I bet he lost his in a nice middle class house in some leafy suburb surrounded by a white picket fence while Charlie Brown was on the TV.

Mind you, let's not get confused with Charlie Manson whose entire virginity-losing experience is best-left unimagined, least cattle and chainsaws come to mind.

I had left School by now and, in order to maintain the newfound independence that having a Scooter afforded me, I needed to earn some money. Full-time employment was never a consideration so I got a job working part-time in a petrol station. Free fuel, parts, and cash in the hand.

Anyone who's ever had a scooter knows what unreliable bastards they are. I had two by now for that very reason, the Lambretta and a Vespa GS – one of them was always off the road. Now that I was mobile I wasn't about to start getting the bus again. Working at the garage helped because it meant I could get hold of some of the more basic bits and pieces and accessories but, unfortunately, nothing major. This wasn't a problem until the day they both broke down at the same time.

I'd recently met a bloke who used the garage from time to time and always seemed to have a different scooter.

It just so happened that he came in when both of mine were busted. We got talking about the bikes and it transpired he was part of a gang that stole them either whole, or for parts, It was a big set up and they apparently did very nicely out of it.

This was about 1970 when Scooters had pretty much died out down south – well, the customized ones certainly had.

This however wasn't the case in the North especially in Manchester; the whole scooter scene was really huge. Kids were still nicking the chrome mirrors off of car doors. Anyway, this bloke told me he could get me the parts I needed for half the price.

I of course declined, thinking "Why do I need you to nick them for me? I can do that for myself thank you very much."

So that's exactly what I did. The very next night, I swiped a Vespa, which was so simple due to the fact that security features on scooters were way down the list of any manufacturers' priorities. Any Vespa key started any other Vespa. The side panels on Lambrettas were unlockable. This meant I was back on the road in no time.

But not for long. The Police had apparently been watching this gang for weeks, biding their time and waiting for right moment to pounce. Which, as luck would have it, was as soon as I was seen riding my scooter with its recently purloined parts. I had also been seen talking to the guy who used the garage, so all of a sudden I was a part of the great scooter-stealing Mob of Manchester, and their number was about to come up.

On a Friday night, they swooped, pulling me over to the side of the road just outside my house, which, I might add now, boasted a backyard so full of scooters and scooter parts that I could have opened a shop. It was instantly and understandably assumed that I was in it up to my neck, especially as the serial numbers on my bike didn't match.

It's a fair cop, Guv. Slap on the irons and take me downtown.

I was accused and arrested for theft, shoved in the back of a Black Maria and whisked away at high-speed, bells ringing, the lot. I naturally tried to offer a hastily thought up excuse to the hard-faced copper sitting opposite me in the van but his only response was to give me a massive punch in the face. Cheers. I didn't say anything after that because the bells ringing in my head were louder than the ones on the fucking roof. When we reached the police station, I was thrown in a cell with two other blokes who looked and smelt as if they'd been in there for some time.

The place stunk of feet and sweat. My cellmates had commandeered both of the hard wooden benches so I tried to get as comfortable as possible curled up in a ball on the floor.

It promised to be a long night. Any thoughts of sleep were banished once the two guys' snoring kicked in.

Suddenly one of them woke up and peered at me with two bloodshot eyes and said, "Do me a favour, kid?"

"What's that, then?" I asked.

"Punch me in the head."

Whaaaat! Now, I'm thinking this bloke is obviously a psycho nutcase who simply wants an excuse to kill me using his bare hands so I politely tell him, "Fuck off, mate. I ain't punching you in the fucking head. Why on earth would you want me to do that?"

Just as I'm finishing my sentence, the other one wakes up and BANG! He punches him right on the chin knocking him out cold. "Fucking hell! What did you do that for?" I ask "The bastard would be up all night if I hadn't." Oh! "He does the same for me if I ask." Nice! Well, as the night crept on he was as good as his word because that was exactly what happened the two of them must have hit each other over a dozen times as calmly as other people shake hands. To say I was a nervous wreck by the time morning finally arrived would be an understatement. My ordeal wasn't over. I was questioned for hours on end all weekend and accused of not only being the gang's ringleader but their obvious mastermind. They also wanted to charge me for over a hundred and fifty nicked scooters.

Luckily, they only managed to connect me to the one Vespa, which I was happy to admit to. I appeared handcuffed in court on the Monday morning looking like shit, was fined two hundred pounds and banned for a year.

I never found out if they rounded up the real scooter-rustlers, but I never saw the guy from the garage anymore, probably because I got the sack as soon as the owner heard I'd been nicked. The police also kept my scooter. I was now out of work, in debt, and a pedestrian. After a few days of feeling sorry for myself, I decided to concentrate my energies on an activity that was close to home which didn't require any transport.

Namely drinking in the local pub, The Broadway.

The Broadway public house on the Broadway in Moston became the centre and focus of my universe. It was typical of a Northern boozer at the time split between Albert Tatlock and Hilda Ogden look-alikes, binmen and labourers. It really was a slice of the times right down to the brassy barmaids, over-filled ash trays, nicotine stains and flock wallpaper, I loved it.

The big album for me at the time was the Faces' A Nod's As Good As A Wink (To A Blind Horse). I remember the kids around the area seemed to be divided into two factions, Faces fans or Slade fans. The main consensus and local attitude (especially in the pub) was that Rod was for poufs because he pranced around in make up and wore a feather boa.

Noddy on the other hand was for geezers: he wore big Doctor Marten boots and came from Wolverhampton. Consequently, there weren't too many kids into the Faces – they were from London and that was worse than anything.

Look, I like Slade as much as the next guy but I always knew the Faces were far cooler. So did my mates. I had a perfect Ian McLagan spiky feather cut, the two-tone shoes and the tartan scarf, and I thought I looked the bollocks. My best mate at the time was a guy called Alan Hughes. He was a few years older, maybe twenty-one. He was into the Faces as well and together we had a bit of respect for the Slade guys in the Broadway because they were a few years older than us plus most of them worked down the local pit and were fucking hard as nails. We would have pint races with them and do a pretty good job of staying up. Alan was a born leader type, the main guy, the sort who was always the life and soul of every party. He also attracted a lot of female attention, because he looked a bit like James Dean.

This was very handy as it meant there was plenty of scope for me copping off with as many of his numerous birds' best mates as I liked. All of which made me feel as if we had it sussed. The Broadway had a jukebox filled with Slade singles that all the Slade lads would mime to every single night.

Come chucking-out time, regular as clockwork, you'd hear these pissed miners, in Noddy-style braces and mutton chops, yelling at the top of their lungs: "Baby, Baby, Bay Beee" or that other chestnut "You Know How Skweeze Me Waaaaaaa' oh." It felt like you was at your uncle's wedding reception.

I'd wanted to be in a band for as long as I can remember (well, since seeing the Beatles) but I had absolutely no idea how to go about it. I would constantly daydream about it every time a great record came out, but then some mundane task would rear its ugly head and I'd put the idea to the back of my mind. Until now! Sitting in that pub watching those karaoke pioneers making an exhibition of themselves finally gave me the inspiration I needed. Why not do it for real?

# CHAPTER TWO
# PART OF
# THE UNION

**ODEON** HAMMERSMITH Tel. 01-748-4081
Manager: Philip Leivers
STRAIGHT MUSIC presents
**BUZZCOCKS**
EVENING 7-30 p.m.
Saturday, Nov. 4th, 1978
**STALLS**
£2·50
BLOCK

22

B30

Losing the job at the garage eventually forced me to face up to the horrible reality that, if I was going to earn my keep at home, pay my fine and, most importantly, finance my renewed musical aspirations, I would alas need to find alternative employment. And so it came to pass that I, Stephen Diggle, reluctantly agreed to take on a full-time job.

Thanks to my Grandad Albert I started work at Mountfords Iron and steel Foundry. Mountfords was a huge Gothic-looking Dickensian metal works on the outskirts of Manchester that looked like it was straight out of the Peter Sellers film I'm Alright Jack. Albert had heard I was a bit stuck for cash and wanted a guitar so he took it upon himself to help me out. Bless him. He was a big trade union man who had a lot of influence at places like Mountfords, so he pulled a few strings and got me in. Now I know it sounds a bit ungrateful, but at the time all I could think was "Oh, Fuck".

I'll never forget how proud he was the next day, as he sat me down and explained how lucky I was and how I was going to be trained as a forge man. This basically meant I was going to work in a furnace that was hotter than the sun, with five other blokes that operated a three-ton hammer, which made the Earth shake! For eight hours a day – oh thanks, I feel really lucky.

My first day was a classic. I'd been there for about three hours, sweating buckets and with that fucking hammer pounding away every few seconds, when all of a sudden we were told to gather round the clocking-in clock. Apparently, some old boy named Len was retiring and I was told he was going to receive a gold watch. "Gold watch?" I enquired. "Yes. son, Ole Len's been here for fifty years! Man and boy, started when he was fifteen years old". Suddenly I was gripped with panic, AAAAA-AAAAAAAAAAhhhhhhhhhhhhhhh! Fifty years of this fucking noise and heat, for a sodding gold watch!

Picture the scene: all the workers were standing impatiently around the big time clock, the clocking-in clock, waiting for old Len to gratefully and tearfully accept his watch from the foreman. I say impatiently because most of the workers preferred to work as piece workers; this meant they got paid for every finished job rather than on the usual hourly rate, i.e. the more you did the more you got paid. Time was money to this lot (some of whom would work right through their breaks literally killing themselves) and Len was costing them, a fact reflected in the magnanimous gift they had all chipped in for.

A tiny portable transistor radio.

I can tell you the whole concept of time wasn't wasted on me, no way. It was chilling, I didn't want money so bad that I would waste all my life clocking in and clocking out in order to get a watch and a radio. Fuck, no! I've got a radio.

I had to get out. In the meantime, I would have to skive to survive. I started straight away. An old favourite was walking quickly around the factory and yard with a very intent look on your face, always carrying something to give the impression that you were actually on some sort of errand and therefore not to be questioned. This would work regularly for a good few hours or until you were knackered at least.

Offering to make the tea was good for losing the odd half hour too, but this one had its drawbacks as workers would break the handles off of the cups and place them back into position with the obvious hilarious results. In the end, I'd thought up so many ways to get out of doing any actual work that it became hard work itself. Eventually, I got bored with the daily ducking-and-diving and took the brazen approach of simply fucking off for hours on end. That did the trick and I soon found myself in the guvnor's office faced with the ultimatum of going on piecework or getting the sack. The guvnor was a great big stocky bastard, a Robert Maxwell-type who would lean over his desk and bear down on you resting on his knuckles. He had no time for this sort of irritation and told me straight: "You do it lad, or you know what you can do". The choice was easy. I'll get me coat. I was out of there in two minutes flat, kicking me heels, a free man at last. There was only one problem, my Granddad!

Obviously, the best course of action was to break the news to him as soon as possible so I went round to his house that lunchtime. Hoping to look suitably crestfallen, I told Albert that Mountford's hard-arsed guvnor had sacked me for refusing to go on to piecework in place of my usual straight wage.

Dumb thing to do. As it turned out, Albert was a good mate of Mountford's shop steward and the next thing I knew I was being dragged round to see him.

I was plonked down in his office and sat in amazement as, between them, they decided that my sacking was somehow against union rules. I didn't like the sound of this and, as my world started spiralling out of control, the rest of the conversation went something along the flustered lines of "Right I want every body out." Oh no, this was war. "No no no! It's fine Granddad I'll get another job" I offered. "No, Steven, he can't sack you for that." "He can, he can." The next day, sure enough, the whole fucking factory was out on strike. I had to walk past every worker in the factory, flanked either side by my uncle and the shop steward, straight into Maxwell's office.

I was reinstated inside a week. "Up the workers". That lasted all of a month, before the same scenario repeated its self, right down to the shop steward wanting to call another walk out. I told him not to bother, as I'll never work again. It was a magical feeling, going home on the bus, and the feeling of freedom. It reminded me of that line from DH Lawrence where he says "go out and discover life." I felt I had done and I didn't fucking like it. So, thankfully, I was eventually sacked successfully. After staying out of my Granddad's way for a while I managed to stay that way.

Free from the unwanted interruption of gainful employment, I decided I'd step up my efforts in forming the group. In order to make ends meet, I sold my other scooter and, with the bit of money saved from Mountfords, I bought a cheap Spanish acoustic guitar and an even cheaper "Antoria" Les Paul copy. I also set up two cassette players so I could record both guitars and then overdub them back onto one cassette! Genius. I even embarked on a bit of DIY and made a little speaker cabinet out of an old wooden box – pretty amazing as I'd never done any woodwork in my life! I even cut a hole in the middle using a chisel and a bit of sandpaper, I'm sure it looked crap but, once it was finished, I really felt as if I was a lot closer to getting it together.

Then disaster struck! After one practically satisfying evening of bedroom practice, I felt a night out was in order. I met up with Alan and the lads down the Broadway and together we got completely pissed. So much so that the guvnor threw us out well before closing time.

Undaunted, we unanimously agreed that our little party should continue elsewhere, and we left the Broadway to the sounds of David Bowie's 'Star Man', bound for a club we knew in Oldham road.

In our drunken state, we'd accepted a lift off of some bloke we barely knew from the pub, who turned out to have a fucking two-door Hillman Imp of all cars. All five of us crammed into anyway: Alan in the front and three in the back with me crushed in the middle. At first, the driver didn't seem to me to be too much the worse for wear, but suddenly I felt the car weave across the road. A near miss came next and then he amazingly let go of the steering wheel in order to light up a fag.

We were now on the wrong side of the road so Alan made a grab for the wheel and tried to steer it from his side. I don't know if the driver passed out at that point but he certainly wasn't helping matters. After swerving violently to the left, we lunged back to the right and hit an oncoming car side on, this sent us careering back to the left and into the car in front. That spun us completely out of control on to a petrol garage forecourt and straight in to the line of pumps. The car finally came to a halt facing the wrong way and filled up with smoke and fumes. We sat there in shock for what could only have been seconds, covered in glass, and blood before sheer panic sat in. I looked up and realized Alan wasn't in his seat and that his door was either wide-open or missing altogether. Then I noticed the driver was missing too. I can only assume some sort of survival instinct took over. We frantically kicked the front seats forwards and miraculously scrambled out. We rolled on to the tarmac and managed to hobble to a safe distance before taking stock of the scene. That's when I grasped the enormity of the crash. Wreckage was strewn everywhere: the Imp's wheels had totally collapsed and the front end was completely gone, along with one of the petrol pumps. Then as the smoke started to clear we noticed Alan lying on the floor some distance away from the car with the driver crouching over him.

Alan looked bad when we got to him, he was obviously unconscious and hurt, but because I'd seen him blind drunk so many times I wasn't instantly concerned. I started to tap his face and lift up his eyelids trying to bring him round when the driver said, "You're wasting your time. He ain't going anywhere. Look at the back of his head." I stopped; turned Alan's head to one side and straightaway understood exactly what he meant: Alan's head was in half! He was stone dead. It was the most horrifying thing I had ever seen: brains, skin, and bone every where. Now the driver's freaking out and shouting, "Oh fuck, what am I ganna do? I've got no fucking tax or insurance."

On top of this witnesses were starting to turn up, so I said to the guy: "Look, mate, I don't even know who you are. You being taxed and insured wouldn't have saved his fucking life anyway. Fucking fags killed him, your fucking fags. You'd better leg it before you're nicked!"

When the police and ambulance eventually arrived we were all patched up, and gave statements saying we hadn't a clue who the driver was. They took Alan's body away and after a check up at the hospital, we were all allowed to go. I can't begin to explain what a profound effect that whole experience had on me; once again, I'd tasted death, only this time much, much closer up. I knew I was lucky to be alive. In some ways, it felt like a miracle. If that petrol station had been open and those pumps active, then we would all have died along with Alan. Heavy reality or, as I would write later, "Some reality". I realized that you had to live for the moment because it could very well be your last. As for the driver, I heard that the police eventually picked him up. I read in the local paper that he got done for manslaughter.

For months afterwards, I would wake up every night, playing the whole thing over and over in my head. Did he save us? Why was he thrown out of the car? And why was he the only one to die? On the day of the funeral, Alan's mum and dad asked me to go in the front car with them and then these words came into my head: "If you know the meaning of death, you know the meaning of life." That's when I vowed I'd form the best fucking band I could and I'd do it for him.

Phase two:

Enter Lance Hartley, the hippie heir to the Hartley's Jam Empire and my next recruit. Lance had dropped out, in order to rebel against his father's fortune and jam in general, when I met him at an Edgar Broughton Band gig at Manchester University. We agreed to form a band with a drummer called Arthur and I moved in to his flat. We set up rehearsals in the living room of what only be described as a total hippie haven, or to give it its correct title "the House of Acid". Lance said he was a bass player but he was useless due to the acid having already finished him off; I believed him though – probably because I was doing about three tabs a day myself. We would do these things called microdots, which were tiny bits of blotting paper with a drop of acid plopped on to it from a little glass eye-dropper.

I found out later it actually had strychnine mixed up in it, but it worked all the same. Lance had all those posters of the time: the naked black chick with the Afro, optical illusions, and that big circle, which looked like it'd been done with a kid's styrograph game. They were like early versions of the magic eye, designs that would appear to move if you stared at them long enough. On one trip, the walls came alive and the face of the Grim

Reaper appeared to be coming for me. Trees chased me too like that scene out of "Snow White", all mind-expanding stuff, or so I thought. I took a whole roll of film photographing the wall, afterwards thinking I'd see that face when they were developed. When I got them back from the chemist, all I had was twelve pictures of wallpaper. After that, I made sure I had better reference material. There was a poster on the living room wall of Manfred Mann's Earth Band, which showed the band holding handfuls of earth. Underneath it read: "This good earth." That's good, I thought, it's grounding. From then on, I would always start a trip looking at that image, whilst listening to Arthur Brown's 'Time Captains' off his Kingdom Come album. Worked a treat. In fact, I told Arthur Brown about it years later, and he told me he understood perfectly?

I got into some serious reading too during this period, especially Aldous Huxley who was like the Irvine Welsh of his day. Brave New World became my guidebook along with Doors of Perception, Gates Of Hell which was all about his experiences with LSD. In it, Huxley theorized that, for the purposes of everyday living, the brain acts like a filter, which allows only essential information to pass through it. Cross the road safely, boil a kettle, or get on the bus: things like that.

He said LSD pushed back this filter, or worked like a key, the key to the door of perception, and once it was opened a torrent of sensations like colours, sounds, and images could flood in. He also predicted a worldwide religious revival would come about if drugs like LSD were freely available. Lance agreed with that one. The thing I liked about him most was that he apparently took a shitload of acid on his deathbed in order to get the most out of what he said would be the ultimate trip. Well, that alone was enough to convince me to start wearing an Afghan coat.

My next highly questionable purchase was a three-wheel Del Boy Trotter van, a Robin Reliant. I'd only just got my licence back at the time and scooters were out. I couldn't afford a real car, so the old Robin was a good alternative. Plus you could drive it on your provisional licence. The only trouble with Robins was you couldn't reverse them. They were irreversible: they didn't have a reverse gear, because they were meant to be driven like a bike. Some genius did actually work out how to adapt it using some sort of metal plate contraption but I never bothered.

You could get a lot of people in them, though; I crammed eight into mine when we went to see Led Zeppelin at Earls Court. Eight people, four bottles of draft Sherry, a bag of Mandrax, a couple of lysergic bottles of acid, and a big bag of Speed. I got the Speed off some guy who didn't have a tooth in his head, not one. The plan was to drive down to London via Nottingham, because someone had said Nottingham had a bird ratio of five-to-one. Nottingham was a college town so it had a ring of truth. Off we went: surf city here we come. When we arrived, we parked in what we thought was a huge deserted car park, and headed for the nearest college hotspots. Five to one or not, I managed to pull a lovely little student bird in the first pub we went to and was doing very nicely thank you. All of a sudden Arthur, who had been liberally helping himself to the on-board refreshments, declares at the top of his voice that he has absolutely no idea who any of us are. He then stands bolt upright and runs straight out the door. Normally, this wouldn't be a problem except Arthur had been nominated as the bagman. So we spent the rest of the evening chasing a man who was literally possessed, running at super human speed, though the streets of Nottingham because seven blokes he'd never seen before in his entire life were chasing him. By the time I got back to the pub, it was shut and there was obviously no sign of the bird so I spent a dejected night trying to sleep sitting upright in a van that now stank of socks and sherry.

If I did manage to drop off, it didn't seem for long because, before I knew it, we were being jolted awake by an almighty banging on the side of the van.

I peered blearily out though the condensation and saw what we originally thought was a car park, was now a full-blown and thriving market place. And we were smack in the middle of it. For what felt like an eternity, I slowly manoeuvred our way through the maze of fruit and veg stalls, running the gauntlet of pissed-off market traders who banged and kicked the side of the van as they threw rotten tomatoes and cabbages at us. If only I could have reversed the fucking thing.

Meanwhile back at the Hartley halls of residence things carried on in much the same vein: the place was still full of tripped-out strangers and people that, quite frankly, smelt bad. Arthur was embroiled in some sort of personal turmoil demanding the answers to such posers as Why Are We Here? And Where Are We Going? (neither of which I could help him with). I lost count of the times I found someone either in my bed, or sitting crying by the side of it. Breakfast was an LSD spiked orange (complete with natural acid) and the band was going nowhere, despite the fact I had actually begun to write songs.

The Beatles had split but their influence over me still lingered on. Thanks to Let It Be, I now understood that the art of songwriting wasn't wizardry or some mystical gift handed down to the chosen few. Playing that album and watching the film showed me that songs didn't, as I once thought, come fully formed.

Here was a band stripped down to basics, jamming and showing you how to write a song. They showed you exactly how it was done and they looked real at last, playing though old amps with beards and singing gobbledegook.

The realization that Lennon made up songs like 'Don't Let Me Down' as he went along blew me away. I saw how he used a string of images, or a stream of consciousness, to supply the lyrics One and One Is Two, Matt Busby, Doris Day, the BBC.

I suddenly thought fucking hell there's no mystery here - I could do that. It's the same as the way Bowie wrote later when he would cut up sentences and rearrange the words. Simple but brilliant. It was all wasted on Lance unfortunately because he had decided to become a Hari Krishna.

I was back to square one.

## CHAPTER THREE
# COUNTDOWN TO YEAR ZERO

**ODEON** HAMMERSMITH **Tel. 01-748-4081**
Manager: Philip Leivers
STRAIGHT MUSIC presents
**BUZZCOCKS**
EVENING 7-30 p.m.
Saturday, Nov. 4th, 1978
**STALLS**
£2·50
BLOCK
22 / B30

These days it's easy to see how far we've come since Punk.

We have the advantage of hindsight for one thing. I find it incredible to think that we now live in an age that is further away in terms of years from when Punk started than we were then to the Beatles breaking up. I think it was Danny Baker that said "It was a ten-year cycle from the summer of love to Sniffin' Glue packing up, 1967 to 1977". He was right. It seemed an age away then, but Sniffin' Glue, the self-styled punk bible, finished only ten years after Sgt Pepper was released, ten years on from the Summer of Love, it was the summer of Punk. We are now almost thirty years on and it's as if it never happened. People have forgotten just how desperate it was living in England during the early seventies.

Fucking hell. Yes were huge then, think about that. It's weird but you've only got to see the newsreels from back then and you can see that England looked like it had literally had the colour washed out of it. You look at the clips of hippies walking down the Kings Road in 1973 and compare them to the hippies going in to the Apple shop in 1967. Or walking down Carnaby Street. You can see the difference and the Seventies had the advantage of better film, didn't it? It sounds stupid but there's a definite difference between Sixties colour and early Seventies colour. It was brutal and heavy in the Seventies and it showed just how styleless England had become. Moustaches and beards had even been cool in the Sixties but, by 1973, they looked shit! People had taken it a beard too far and they were lost.

I include myself here, hence the acid, or LSD, or what ever else was knocking around. Like everybody else, I was tripping out, hoping to find somewhere better – escape reality more like, or to find out who I was – but then I realized, hang on! I know exactly who I am, and actually there isn't anywhere else to go – well, I could have got a tambourine and a bed sheet and followed Lance down Oxford Street, I suppose. I couldn't believe how far I'd let myself get carried away by all that shit. I'd come from birds, booze, and scooters to loons, a granddad shirt and a feeling that I was in One Flew Over The Cuckoo's Nest. Fucking hell! Did I need to wake up and rediscover my roots! Anyway, it was no use tripping out while the gas bill was poking you in the ribs, which was something Lance never seemed to worry about. There was no doubt the entire hippie ethic had to go. I mean, if I were to remain a worthwhile statistic amongst the nation's one million unemployed, I needed to be surrounded by people like me, musicians. And there was only one place to go: The Free Trade Hall. To watch… er… Patrick Moraz. Who? Well, Patrick Moraz, believe it or not, was Rick Wakeman's replacement in Yes, a man who was quite obviously deluding himself and going out solo. This guy had a fucking shop's worth of keyboards, banks and banks of them, with all those jackplug socket boards that looked like a telephone exchange. It was ridiculous, but that wasn't all, half way though a number he jumped up and blew into a 15-foot Alpine horn. That's when I knew I'd been had. It probably would have sounded all right if I'd been stoned, but now I could see and hear it for the rubbish it was. I wanted to hear a power chord; I wanted Meaty Beaty Big And Bouncy, Doctor Martens and a boiler suit.

My group's next incarnation involved a guy who lived around the corner from my parents called Jack Ball. He was the brother of my sister's best mate and he played bass. We had a drummer whose name escapes me, but I remember he eventually ran off with Jack's wife, which, I thought, was very rock'n'roll. We were very rough but we did master a few old chestnuts, 'Paranoid' and 'Brown Sugar', that sort of thing.

I also learnt to play using open tuning like Keith Richard, using only the one finger in open G simply because it was so much easier than the awkward conventional six-string tuning, but also because my guitar was a piece of crap. I still had the shitty Les Paul copy, which I played though my little homemade speaker. By now I was, if I do say so myself, actually quite good. However, if I was to reach the next rung of the ladder, I desperately needed better equipment. So I went cap in hand and asked my Dad who said he'd see what he could do. He was a lorry driver at the time, delivering stuff all over the North. As luck would have it, a shipment of guitars was due in from the States. Luckily for me, Dad decided that they surely wouldn't miss one and pinched me what he thought was a good one, a Hyman. When I got home that night, he said to me, "there's a guitar upstairs, son. Go up and have a look".

I belted up the stairs opened the box. Sure enough, there was a brand spanking new… bass. My Dad came up after and said, "What do you think, son?" "Er… it's a bass, Dad!" Puzzled look. "It's a bass. It only has four strings!" Puzzled look. "A guitar has six strings." More puzzled look. "It's fantastic, Dad! Thanks."

Then as I sat there looking at that bass, it suddenly dawned on me: wait a minute! This could work to my advantage! Every Tom, Dick and Harry wants to be the guitar player.

Every time I look in the Manchester Evening News, all the ads are from guitarists wanting bass players. They all want to be guitar heroes, never the bass player. There must be a genuine shortage of bass players. That's it! That's the answer. If you want to get regular work, as a musician, then be the fucking bass player. Join someone else's band and let them do all the hard work. It certainly made sense in my case, especially as Jack's wife had just brought about the premature ending to yet another group. Sod it; I'm putting an ad in tomorrow.

The best paper at the time was the Manchester Review, which was like Time Out, so I picked up a copy first thing in the morning. As it happens, I didn't even have to put myself out that much, because there were so many requests for bass players, all I had to do was reply to one. Top of the list read: "Guitarist forming band, needs bass player". "That'll do me," I thought, so I rang the number and spoke to the would-be Jeff Beck on the other end. To give him his due, he sounded quite cool. I told him I wanted to be in a band like The Who, smash things up and play R'n'B, which meant absolutely no hippie bollocks. He said great. All right, then, let's meet outside the Free Trade Hall, tomorrow night Friday, the fourth of June.

A brief history lesson:

The year is 1976 and Britain is basking in the hottest summer it's seen in over a century. Harold Wilson has quit as prime minister, convinced he's the target of a MI5 spy ring. Supersonic air travel began as two Concordes took off simultaneously from London and Paris, while Moscow officials issued thousands of posters proclaiming Margaret Thatcher the wicked cold war witch. Oh yes, and Dame Agatha Christie died. As a mark of respect, the lights on the St Martin's Lane theatre in London (where the Mousetrap is in its fortieth year) were dimmed, less than a hundred yards along the road from St Martin's Collage of Art. It was there in January that a group of four spiky misfits by the names of Johnny Rotten, Glen Matlock, Steve Jones and Paul Cook had played a ramshackle set in January. Collectively they were known as The Sex Pistols and according to an elitist group of art school trendsetters and their bored suburbanite entourage, they were the future of rock and roll. In February, the band played support at the legendary Marquee club, blowing away headliners Eddie And The Hot Rods and destroying the PA system with a chair. Their small but frantic following called themselves the Blank Generation and looked like a wild mutation, with traces of glam rock decadence mixed in with S+M drag. They were the angry little brothers and sisters of Bowie and Roxy fans, too young to have witnessed either while they still processed any ounce of cool. Tits were frequently on show, hair dyed jet-black, T-shirts purposely ripped and safety pins were a must-have costume and facial accessory. "Don't look over your shoulder, but the Sex Pistols are coming!" screamed the New Musical Express the following week. They were right. Within a few short months the Pistols whipped up the sort of mass hysteria that we reserve nowadays for child killers, dead princesses and Osama Bin Laden. They defaced and ridiculed the Queen, got banned from Radio One, and ensured at least one TV presenter got the sack, i.e. a pissed-up Bill Grundy. They also recorded one of the seminal rock albums of all time, Never Mind The Bollocks Here's The Sex Pistols, which took them to number one and reputedly made them a million. It was decadent majesty on a grand sneering scale and it wasn't lost on a whole slew of wannabe rockers, or as they came to be known punk rockers. Some of the Pistols own suburbanite devotees had even broken away from the collective known as "The Bromley Contingent" in a bid to grab some personal notoriety and attention by reinventing themselves. Little Susan Janet Dallion, went all Rocky Horror Show (complete with dubious swastika armbands), and formed the ridiculously amateurish Siouxsie And The Banshees with herself in the lead role as Siouxsie Sioux. Young William Broad perfected an unfortunate Cliff Richard, top-lip snarl and morphed into Billy Idol, the peroxide pouting front man of cartoon punks Generation X. Steve Bailey became Steve Severin, one of the Banshees. Ray Burns, who came from Croydon near Bromley, became the non-commissioned Captain Sensible. And so on and so forth. Not every punk rocker came from the wrong bend in the cul-de-sac, though: some even came from council estates. Simon Ritchie, for example: he became Sid Vicious. Marion Elliott was, of course, Poly Styrene. Nor did they all adopt a suitable "Wild One" nom de plume, like Rat Scabies or indeed Johnny Rotten. Some just formed punk rock bands with punk rock band names: like barman Shane McGowan who formed The Nipple Erectors and postal worker Mick Jones who formed The Clash.

Two characters who did go the whole hog were Peter McNeish, and Howard Trafford. McNeish and Trafford were friends from The Bolton Institute of Technology, avid Velvet Underground fans, and both experimenting with music. McNeish was taking a HND course at the Institute, running the music society, and playing periodically with his old school band, Jets Of Air. They met when Trafford joined the society, requiring musical help with a electronic video project he was working on. When Jets Of Air split, McNeish joined Trafford in an unnamed group project after reading an advert he'd posted on the Institute's noticeboard. Trafford had asked for people to form a group in order to do a version of the Velvets' 'Sister Ray'. Various other musicians also auditioned but, in the end, it all came to nothing and the idea was scraped. Nevertheless, McNeish and Trafford decided to stick together, especially after reading

Neil Spencer's review of the Sex Pistols gig at the Marquee. Both had been impressed to read that the Pistols had covered, amongst other personal favorites, an Iggy and the Stooges' cover as well as self-penned numbers with titles like 'I'm Pretty Vacant'. The review described the band as "a musical experience, with the emphasis on experience," quoting Rotten as saying "we're not into music, we're into chaos". It was all the motivation McNeish and Trafford needed to arrange a trip down to London in order to see this experience for themselves. Trafford had a friend called Richard Boon, who was studying Art at Reading University, close enough to London for a weekend visit on the off chance of catching the Pistols live. The duo borrowed a car and duly arrived at Boon's, presumably without calling ahead: one flick though their host's copy of Time Out magazine showed no listings for the group. It did, however, have a review of the truly woeful Thames Television series called Rock Follies which starred Julie Covington, Rula Lenska and, er... the quiet one, playing an all-girl rock band, very badly. The episode in question was described as "It's a buzz, cock!" Inspired Carry On-style, Trafford spliced the two last words of the sentence together and turned them into punk's first double entendre "Buzzcocks", a bloody good name for a band. It actually means sod all, but you know what you think of when you hear it right?

Of course, "a vibrator". Oh boy, that's as good as a Sex Pistol, that is. Who were actually playing the following night, after all. A call to the NME had put the three friends in touch with the band's manager, ex-New York Dolls Svengali and clothes shop proprietor, Malcolm McLaren. He'd told them about two gigs that very weekend, the first at High Wycombe's College Of Further Education and the following night at Welwyn Garden City. McNeish and Trafford attend both shows and are so blown away that they arrive back in Manchester with their very own nom de plumes. Peter McNeish is now Pete Shelley (his mother's choice, if he'd been born a girl) and Howard Trafford has become Howard Devoto (the surname of a Cambridge bus driver his philosophy teacher had told him about). The vehicle for the pair's new identities is "Buzzcocks" and new recruits are needed. Shelley brings in Garth Davies, the former bass player with Jets Of Air, and the three rehearse for a planned debut at the Bolton Institute Of Technology scheduled for the first of April. Even without a drummer, a full set is worked up containing several of Shelley's old Jets Of Air compositions, including 'Love You', 'Sixteen Again' and 'Homosapien'. In order to play the gig (a social evening arranged by the institute's textile students), the group drafted in Phil Lenoir, drummer with local heroes Black Cat Bones, the heavy rock outfit that got Paul Kossoff off the starting blocks. They opened their set with a cover of David Bowie's 'Diamond Dogs' and closed it one song later when the organisers pulled the plugs on a particularly shambolic version of Chuck Berry's 'Come On'. Undeterred, Shelley and Devoto vow to carry on and devise a plan to support the Sex Pistols.

Inspired by an astute Richard Boon, who had already booked the Pistols to play at Reading University himself, Shelley and Devoto book the Pistols to play Manchester's lesser Free Trade Hall – a small club space above the bigger Free Trade Hall – for the princely sum of thirty-two pounds. Unfortunately, Lenoir and Davies have other ideas – such as leaving. An emergency ad is placed in the New Manchester Review, asking for a drummer and bass player, once again stressing the importance of the Velvet Underground and Bowie influences. It's academic, though: there's not enough time between auditions and the event to assemble a new Buzzcocks line-up. A group called the Mandela Band from nearby Blackburn is brought in at the last minute as replacement. Disappointed, Shelley and Devoto make do with collecting tickets (fifty pence a pop) and working the lights.

# CHAPTER FOUR
# "IT'S THE BUZZ, COCK!"

ODEON HAMMERSMITH Tel. 01-748-4081
Manager: Phillip Leivers
STRAIGHT MUSIC presents
BUZZCOCKS

EVENING 7-30 p.m.
Saturday, Nov. 4th, 1978

STALLS
£2·50

BLOCK

22

B.30

41

It's Friday the forth of June 1976. Around fifty punters are queuing up to see the Sex Pistols play the furthest north they've ever ventured. The venue is Manchester's Lesser Free Trade Hall, and the group's manager Malcolm McLaren is outside hustling kids in off the street.

I had no idea who was playing when I turned up at the place, I was just there to meet the guitar player from the ad. Quite a few people were going in or, should I say, being coaxed in by this strange-looking fella in a Teddy boy drape jacket, leather trousers and brothel creepers. What happened next was either the strangest of coincidences or an act of fate. To this day, I can't decide which. I asked him who was on and he said it's The Sex Pistols. "Oh, what are they like?" I asked. "They're like the Who." Fucking hell, really? "Yes, they do 'Substitute'. Are you coming in?" Then I told him I couldn't because I was waiting for this guitarist to turn up from an advert I'd rung in the Manchester Review and suddenly he seemed to know all about it. He said, "Oh, are you a bass player, then? The guitarist is inside collecting tickets." I followed him inside. I'm thinking: I don't remember this arrangement. I thought we were meeting outside and going down the pub. It transpires Shelley had also arranged to meet another bass player who had answered his advert in the paper and Malcolm was keeping an eye out for him. I don't know this yet so Malcolm introduces me to Shelley in the ticket box and we agree to meet in the bar a bit later. I wait to see the Pistols. The place is really empty. Lucky if there were fifty people in. Which didn't look very promising, especially as the place was an all-seater venue. All you could see were just the odd groups of heads sitting down the front in the first three rows. I sat at the back not knowing what to expect other than a version of 'Substitute' when all of a sudden the Pistols just ambled on. There was Rotten with bright yellow teeth. Straightaway, he's spitting, and fuck this and fuck that. Steve Jones is thrashing his guitar, making this almighty racket. Matlock and Cook were so fucking loud but just brilliant together: honestly, forget any of those stories about the Pistols not being able to play. I hadn't seen or heard anything like it in my life. This was fast and furious. I was totally transfixed and knew there wasn't anything like them in the whole country. England was indeed fucking dreaming at that time and this was its wake-up call.

I felt I had come alive that night. I could feel the power of the music, and it made me think. Here at last was a band that was saying something relevant. If you didn't like it, they didn't care. I think I was still a bit stunned by the time Shelley found me in the bar but I remember thinking he looks like he's part of all this. He had little spindly legs in these summer pink trousers, which were old loons dyed and taken in to make drainpipes, a homemade T-shirt and some sort of see-though top. I didn't think he looked particularly cool but he did look different. You have to remember there were no straight trousers available in 1976. Every clothes shop back then was a sea of denim and cheesecloth. People would point at you at the bus stop if you had straight trousers on. In fact, that's exactly what struck me about early punk: it was a style that seemed really new and really exciting yet it was drawing heavily on some of my own Sixties influences. The Pistols had even done Small Faces and Monkees numbers. Fuck, I wanted to get in a band like that.

I started recounting the phone conversation I thought Shelley and I had had the previous night about how I wanted to be in a band like The Who and smash things up. At first, Shelley seemed to still be in agreement. He told me he wanted to do classic three-minute pop songs (which was good), play them really loud (that's good, too) and fast (even better). But then he started going over some of the things he had said to who ever he'd spoken to the night before, which obviously wasn't me. The Velvet Underground? David Bowie? Love songs? When he got to Nico, the penny dropped. I thought, I never said a fucking word of this. Then Devoto appeared. He looked more way out than Shelley: he had receding hair even then but he'd dyed it bright red, he wore a bit of eyeliner and some sort of taken-in, pin-striped number. They were both a bit camp and a little bit seedy but they complemented each other in a way that felt right. They had a bit of the Pistols look going and seemed to be very clued up. After witnessing what I'd seen that night, that was very appealing indeed. Devoto asked me if I could rehearse on the Sunday. I jumped at the chance. At that moment, someone asked us if any one was meant to be meeting a guitar player outside. I quickly denied any knowledge of such an arrangement and shuffled Shelley and Devoto up to the bar so we could exchange phone numbers. As I left the Free Trade Hall I noticed a couple of musician types talking and swapping phone numbers outside and wondered, could they have been our original contacts? Who knows? They might have become the fucking Smiths for all we know.

Shelley and Devoto both lived in flats down the same street, Lower Broughton Road, Shelley at number 380, and Devoto at 364. The rehearsal was at Devoto's. The first thing I noticed when I got in there was a huge Monitor lizard stuck in a fish tank. I thought it was plastic to begin with because it didn't move – well, not until we playing, it didn't. We were all plugged into the one amp – Shelley on guitar, Devoto singing, and me on bass – when suddenly this fucking luminous green thing leapt out of the tank and started running around the room, hissing and fucking spitting at us! Despite that, there was a good chemistry right from the first note. It was incredible because none of us really knew each other that well, me least of all. Somehow, we connected. It was defiantly there. I think it stemmed from all three having experienced the Pistols. The feeling that you don't need money, you just need ideas. That's what I think we took from it. We worked on about six or seven originals which really impressed me. I had some songs but I was still figuring most of them out. They had stuff already finished, things like 'Boredom' and 'Orgasm Addict', which seemed fantastic to me and dissimilar from what the Sex Pistols were doing. These were fast, stabby songs that spat at you. I mean, 'Orgasm Addict' is inspired writing, a classic. I was writing a lot but in a completely different way to those guys, a different style altogether. I had 'Fast Cars' which went on the first album but that's all I had which I felt fitted in. That first rehearsal was all it took. I was in. I was a Buzzcock. Now all we needed was a drummer.

Enter John Maher: sixteen years of age and already one of the best drummers I'd ever heard. John had been unsuccessfully trying out for bands around Manchester as a guitar player and only switched to drums about six weeks prior to joining us.

We very nearly had a girl drummer. Devoto had rung some drummer's advert in Melody Maker or somewhere, and it turned out to be a girl. She couldn't make it and put him onto John. He'd only had his kit for about a week. Fuck knows where he got it from: a whole kit was expensive and he was only a spotty little school kid. In fact, he was still doing his exams when we met him. We were so desperate to get going that Devoto gave him the gig without ever hearing him play. That was a pretty good gamble because he turned out to be phenomenal. He picked up the songs in no time.

He was a natural and very inventive he used to have this thing like a coalscuttle that he would use as a crash cymbal. It sounded fantastic. It made a really mad noise, a weird crack.

We never gave a thought to the fact he was underage and therefore legally too young to play anywhere. The line-up was complete. We moved John's kit into the bed-sit and we rehearsed every day – until Devoto's neighbour couldn't stand it any longer. He was the caretaker at St Boniface's Church. He let us use the church hall for nothing just so he wouldn't have to hear us. I don't know who was more grateful.

Shelley's original plan to support the Pistols was back on again – this time they booked the bigger Free Trade Hall because they were getting more well known. John left school and was supposed to take a job at the Methodist Insurance Company but he never went, so we could rehearse solidly for about three weeks. Devoto would ride down to the off licence on his pushbike and bring back a big bottle of cider, which was passed around between songs. Ah! the glamour of it all.

The big night was Tuesday the 20th of July. We were told that all these big name journalists were coming up from London with the Pistols: Sounds, New Musical Express, the whole fucking lot. Before the gig, Shelley and me went out to Pizza Hut and got drunk on a few carafes of wine and smoked a lot of Rothmans – incidentally, the band's cigarette of choice. We walked back to the Free Trade Hall. As soon as we walked though the door, there was a lift right in front of us. It opened and there were the Sex Pistols, looking completely fucked-up: they had all these safety pins hanging off their coats, mad spiky hair, beer tins and those same yellow teeth. They were so drunk that they all fell out of the lift right in front of us all in a big heap. An amazing sight. It was like "fucking hell! That's the future, right there!" Suddenly, I didn't feel drunk enough. The journalist rumour turned out to be true too. They were all there: Neil Spencer, Nick Kent, Lester Bangs – all trying to get an angle on something that they weren't quite sure about. They knew something was happening or was bubbling under at ground level and they could feel the tide was turning but it didn't have a label yet. And there it was a drunken laughing heap on the floor covered in beer and still looking sensational.

Suddenly it was gig time. I think we went on either before Slaughter and the Dogs or after them. I don't remember. What I do remember is the fucking nerves. We were all fired up with this incredible nervous energy. We raced on the stage and just spat those songs out as fast as we could. The nerves controlled the whole thing. It was pure adrenalin mixed with anger at trying to get all this stuff across. Every song we played was at twice the normal tempo as conventional rock songs. We knew that what we had was unique. It was a new sound. That made it frustrating, knowing we quite possibly sounded terrible because our equipment was crap. We had all this homemade shit. It was ridiculous when you think about it because nobody would do that now. It certainly didn't do us justice but that was the spirit of it. Shelley had bought this little Woolworth's guitar, which was the poxiest thing on earth. It all looked tacky and sounded terrible but it had terrible beauty, too. All this energy just poured out of us and into the crowd – to such an extent that it seemed the gig lasted all of two minutes. We spat our heads off for ten songs or however many we did and that was it. Shelley smashed his guitar to bits and the audience went crazy. The atmosphere was electric. They were all jumping about and actually setting the scene for what was to come. I couldn't afford to smash anything so I just threw my bass into the PA and hoped for the best. Then, without thinking, I jumped off the stage, followed by John who leapt over his kit into the crowd. We both ran though the audience straight up to the bar. They couldn't understand it. They thought it was weird because they were so used to seeing bands finish their set and disappear to the dressing room. We felt we were a part of them, but we had also gone and done our bit as well. The natural thing to do afterwards was to go and drink with them and watch the Pistols.

Apart from playing the actual gig, it was probably the best thing we could have done: it was a home gig, a Manchester crowd and they realized we were all local lads. Ninety per cent of the people in there were locals. Every one of them knew the Pistols were going to be a really big deal but, at the end of the day, they were Londoners. It was like a light coming on: now here was a Manchester band who was no different to them. Fucking hell! We didn't have to put our hands in our pockets once. That was the greatest feeling, getting drunk with the punters, watching the Pistols and then getting the bus home.

I walked from the Free Trade Hall and stood in the bus queue with all the kids I'd been at the gig with and stood at the bar with. They were all saying, "This is amazing" and patting me on the back. I could tell that they had all got it, they understood what it was all about and what we and the Pistols were trying to do. The message was "DO IT YOURSELF!" We had made our gear, we'd played our songs and we'd had a powerful impact. I can't emphasize how important it was for those kids at that time, how important it was for music in this country. Before all that happened, everyone (including me) was blagging in to see spoilt brats with ten grand's worth of synthesisers who'd bore you to tears, Chris Squire driving past in a limo watching the television. It was impossible to conceive, if you worked in a steelworks, how you could get to where he is. It was quite simply unobtainable, until then! There were a million people on the dole and here were bands that were saying "Get up off your arse. Express yourself. You too can do it." They were all relating to it. The barrier had gone between the ordinary kid on the street and the musician on the stage.

We had this old Jamaican guy called Augustus who'd sort of roadie for us – we got him out of a newsagent's window: "Van and driver for hire". He would pick up our gear, set up the stage and then take it all home for us afterwards. He was one of those classic laid-back Rasta types always smoking a spliff, always stoned. He would always ask the same questions: "Hey, man, whet's happening?" and "What do you call that music, man?" He would always ask us what the lowdown was and then never listen to a word you said.

That old van was so fucking noisy, it would rattle and shake you to bits. We'd be in the back shouting over the noise. Augustus used to get a tenner a gig. His parting shot was always "Hey, you never know one day it might happen for you guys." Then he would disappear into the night. But I'm jumping ahead of myself.

We were all on a high for a week or two following the Free Trade Hall: we'd played our first gig and had our first mention in the press (I think it was in Sounds. The review said we were rubbish but that didn't bother us: Shelley bought every copy in the paper shop). Ambitions were high. We were determined to get out there and show people just what we could do, even if it was in a biker's pub in Staley Bridge. Which is exactly where our next gig was. It was at The Commercial Hotel, a famous rockers' hang out on the outskirts of Manchester.

We rattled up to the place. There to greet us was a row of about a hundred motorbikes, lined up outside. As you might imagine, this didn't bode well. We all had fluorescent green socks on, Devoto had orange hair and Shelley's looking as camp as a row of tents and wearing a pair of red carpet slippers. This place was full to the rafters with hairy-arsed bikers whose only interest was to get drunk, fart and listen to Steppenwolf. We were booked to do two twenty-minute sets and opened up with 'Orgasm Addict'. The silence was deafening. We decided we'd race though the first twenty minutes without stopping, have a quick break, do the same again, and then get the fuck out of there. I was even working out the chords to 'Born To Be Wild'.

We finished the first set and looked out at the crowd who by now were staring at us as if we had just landed from another planet. Not a soul moved, every single one of them just stood there stone-faced, not even flinching.

I honestly thought, "That's it. It was a short career, Steve, and now you're going to get slaughtered with a bike chain."

Just then the landlord came up to us and said, "Well, that was great. I'm sure everyone really enjoyed it, but there's really no need for you guys to go back on. Here's your money. I suggest you leave as quickly as you can. Good luck".

I think the fact that the landlord was a woman saved our lives because she sort of soothed the savage beast, so to speak.

She intervened on the crowd's behalf and basically got us out in one piece, that and the fact the bikers had absolutely no idea what the fuck they'd just witnessed. By the time they did, we were all in the back of Augustus's old Bedford, fifteen quid better off, shouting over the noise and sharing his joint.

Our association with Malcolm McLaren and the Pistols strengthened and thankfully it became an ongoing thing, the band were fast becoming the biggest thing on Fleet Street and therefore the country. McLaren to his credit didn't forget the small part we'd played in their build up. The first big leg-up he gave us was to invite us down to London for our very first photo shoot. It was for a bizarre French teenage magazine called Bravo, as famous for printing as much nudity as for its music coverage. It was a kind of latter day Loaded, only French – or possibly German – and I suppose it was very ahead of its time, and for that matter very punk. The deal was to turn up at the Notre Dame Hall, which is just off of Leicester Square, and make it look like we were playing a proper gig for a photo spread entitled "Punk Rock" – incidentally, the first time I'd heard the phase mentioned or seen it in print. Anyway, the Pistols had all their gear set up: I couldn't believe it. They mimed for the photographer. Very professionally, I might add, but they fucking mimed, posing and doing the whole bit. It was ridiculous. I mean they had all their stuff set up yet they weren't going to play a note. I wasn't having any of that. We set up our stuff and played a whole set live. It got us our first picture in the New Musical Express. Next up was another support to the Pistols, this time on their home turf. We were first on at the Screen On The Green, a cinema in Islington, north London. It was partly offered to us as a return gesture by McLaren who was really into building a scene and getting the pecking order established right from the start. He had the Clash on the same bill, which was basically their debut outing apart from a couple of behind-closed-doors affairs for the press. We arrived and straight away you could feel the buzz in the air, sitting in the van with our cheap cider and seeing those names up there: Pistols, Clash and Buzzcocks. It just looked so bizarre. The night before we were playing a fucking pub in Stalybridge.

It suddenly started to make a lot more sense to me. This was where we belonged. I just never knew it. It was as if this was the crystallization of punk rock in England. Without even trying, I was smack in the middle of it. Of course, we had no fucking idea who the Clash were but the name fit perfectly. One of those band names that always looks good written down.

The very first person we bumped into getting out of the van was a guy wearing a black suit jacket with a white shirt covered in paint. Instead of a jacket pocket, he had a broken vanity mirror in its place. I thought, "That looks crap," but there was something about him that screamed "Rock Star". He was cocksure. He turned to us and, without being asked, said, "Alright?

I'm Mick Jones and I'm in the Clash". Oh, okay then, that's got that one sorted out. The place was filling up but it was nowhere near full by the time we were on. We were the first band on and any idea of punk solidarity soon vanished.

The London crowd wasn't interested in a bunch of Northern oiks, and they let us know it. They weren't all standing there, demanding to be entertained. Some got into it but it was a frosty reception nonetheless. I hit Devoto with my bass a few times, quite unintentionally, while he was singing. The audience seemed to like that. So that became a bit of a regular thing. It was something that came out of the band's chemistry and it spoke to them. It looked as if we were against each other and that was a way of expressing it. It was really more to do with having no stage experience and it would drive him mad. We were definitely excluded from proceedings that night, but that didn't stop me soaking it all up and totally enjoying it, albeit from a slightly cynical angle. I caught on from the very start that the Clash and, to a lesser extent, the Pistols, were pure show business. They were unbelievably cool and had the style. You could tell they'd spent a lot of time in front of the mirror getting the look right. All of them had Vivienne Westwood outfits or stuff designed by Jamie Reid or some other Art school toff. I never knew all this at the time but you knew they weren't getting that gear down the high street.

It's the equivalent of a band nowadays having their stuff designed by Stella McCartney. And they got that stuff for nothing! Okay, the Clash might have painted on the odd boiler suit themselves – I know Simenon did – but it was still well worked-out showbiz.

We couldn't afford King's Road chic. We came from Manchester where the top designs came from Marks and Spencer and C&A. My brother used to go to college and he'd get me a pinstripe suit jacket for thirty pence. Mind you, it fucking well showed up the difference: one review said we looked like orphans.

Despite my initial reservations about the Clash, I was well and truly hooked on them. Mick interested me the most because he seemed to have the same musical influences as me. He was steeped in the classics: the Stones, Mott the Hoople, and even Elvis, all of which presented him with big contradiction problems later on, once the punk manifesto had been carved in stone. He was from the traditional school of rock stars. He belonged in Keith Richard's class, along with Mick Ronson and Ron Wood. He wouldn't have been out of place poncing a fag off of those guys.

Another lesson we learnt from our first London experience was the importance of having a manager. We saw how McLaren was steering the Pistols on to bigger and better things, how Bernie Rhodes was pulling strings for the Clash. They were getting the right journalists on their side, people like Caroline Coon and Tony Parsons who were writing pages and pages of favourable editorial and glowing gig reviews. Our only mention following the Screen gig was in Sounds and that said we sounded "rougher than a bear's arse".

We elected Richard Boon to do the honours. Together with his friend Sue Cooper, he created New Hormones management. His first job was to collect the door money at our next gig at Holdsworth Hall, back home in Manchester. Eater, a London group who had some spotty fifteen-year-old singer (who'd never played a gig in his life) were booked to support. Unknown to me, Shelley had agreed to toss a coin with this kid to see who would actually headline. He'd lost, so unbelievably they end up following us. They got canned off after three numbers: just deserts! Aside from that bit of North/South rivalry, it was a pretty low-key event, attracting no press coverage. This was possibly due to the real action taking place back in London at The 100 Club Punk Festival.

Unbelievable as it seems now, things really had moved that fast. Punk was now big enough to warrant its own two-night affair in the heart of the West End. The Pistols and the Clash had headlined the first night; the second night was to feature as many punk rock bandwagon-jumpers as possible: we were headlining. I sensed that the Clash had already shifted up an almighty gear; that, in the great scheme of things, they had the potential to become the scene's front-runners. I felt we had our work cut out for us if we were to keep a respectable distance between us and what was fast becoming a fucking deluge of bands, all jostling for the spotlight. The brilliant punk fanzine Sniffin' Glue was now on issue four. Its editor-in-chief Mark Perry had called for more punk bands to form. That in itself was a good thing, but fucking hell we didn't need the far-too-many that did. Siouxsie and the Banshees had made their debut on the Monday along with Subway Sect; The Vibrators, a band who clearly thought they'd gone one better than us namewise, joined us on the Tuesday. We also had a French outfit called Stinky Toys on our bill. They had a big fat bird dressed like a prison warder who screamed out versions of Bowie's 'Hang On To Yourself' and the Stones' 'Under My Thumb'. The one saving grace on an otherwise dreadful night was the Damned who were like the fancy dress turn. Unsurprisingly, everything ran over time on the night, thanks to punch-ups, bottle-throwing, and some lengthy string changing. This was topped off by an especially long and unscheduled jam session featuring Chris Spedding, some Vibrators and Captain Sensible. As the clock ticked away we knew we'd been stitched up.

By the time we managed to get on stage, it was getting very close to last train home time. We ploughed through the set for the benefit of those that risked the night bus and left the stage with Shelley's guitar feeding back at ear-splitting level. It wasn't a total waste of time, though. Sniffin' Glue gave us our first mention and wrote us up a good little review, which likened us to the Pistols. It also said Shelley's guitar "was a spitting rasping monster" and the Vibrators were the worst band of the whole two days. The contrast between the 100 Club and our next gig couldn't have been greater.

We'd agreed to play a free gig for the St. Boniface's Church youth club, by way of appreciation for all the rehearsal time they'd given us. What we didn't know was the average age of the kids that used the club was roughly eight. We'd just set everything up when they started to arrive along with their mums. Suddenly the place was full of these little kids all whooping and shrieking and running around like mad. 'Orgasm Addict' was obviously out of the question as was 'Peking Hooligan', 'Love Battery' and, as for 'Oh Shit!' … I think we were down to about six numbers by the time we worked out a suitable set list.

We put down our first recordings the following week in a little loft studio in Bramwell Lane, Stockport. We ran though the entire set live for a cost of £45. The studio's engineer, Andy MacPherson, recorded and mixed it all in under four hours, finishing it off at his flat to save money. It sounded pretty good to me and certainly good enough for somebody to bootleg it on the "Time's Up" album about a year later.

Richard's first independent decision as our manager came following our free gig at St. Boniface's. He decided to change our rehearsal facility, and moved us from the Church Hall to Lifeline, a drug rehabilitation centre on lower Mosely Street. It was November by now and you could tell most of the centre's inhabitants considered Christmas had come early by the way they eyed up our gear.

So now we have to load up the van, set up and play, and then take it all back down afterwards. You couldn't take your eyes off of it for a minute. And now we also have to take it all home with us, too. Nice one, Rich.

The next big events in the Buzzcocks' evolution were playing The Electric Circus, (where I met Ian Curtis) and getting our first positive review in the New Musical Express. The NME said: "The Buzzcocks are producing the most significant musical output of any new British rock band. Where they're going to go next is anyone's guess!"

Where we were going was on the now-infamous Sex Pistols' Anarchy Tour. We weren't originally booked to play, as I think Malcolm thought he'd already paid us back for our initial help and now they didn't need it. The Pistols were well on their way to number one, and he had chains of London bands all up for support. The Damned were now moving up the food chain. They were the first group pencilled in. We were going to go along regardless because we knew them, and then we found out we were on the bill almost on the day of the gig. Their shows were forever being cancelled at the time so it was always touch-and-go whether it would take place. Their date in Derby the previous week had been cancelled because they had a proviso that Derby Borough Council had insisted the Pistols perform for them first, in private. The idea was for all the Council dignitaries and local committee members to decide whether the band was deemed suitable for public exposure. Such was the country's paranoia with punk rock; they didn't want to be held responsible for corrupting the city's youth. One of the things on the agenda was to also find out if it was true what they'd read, that punk audiences showed their appreciation by spitting at the groups while they played. Ah yes, gobbing, the downside of the live experience: it was absolutely fucking disgusting. It had supposedly started at a Pistols gig in London after Rotten allegedly spat at a crowd member. He's never denied his sinus problem but whether it's responsible for the tidal wave of phlegm that followed is debatable. Still, something started it. By December 1976, it was pretty widespread. As were some of the repercussions. I remember Siouxsie got gobbed in the eye at some gig and ended up with conjunctivitis and had to wear a surgical eye patch. Joe Strummer even ended up hospitalised with hepatitis after involuntarily swallowing pints of audience spit. No, it wasn't good. Luckily, the lead singer bore the brunt of it. They would be forever threatening to walk off, Shelley included.

We only got it a few times, because we handled it differently and the kids could see we weren't into it. If enough of it got you, it would take the colour out of your shirt. Shelley used to say, "Don't gob at me! You don't gob at your record player, do you? Save it for the fucking Damned!" They were the ones that really encouraged it. I did get one in my mouth once, fucking vile, I couldn't help but swallow it because it went straight down the back of my throat as I was singing. I was green for the rest of the gig. Another time I had a particularly gruesome one hit the neck of my guitar. It was a bright yellow glowing bastard. We were playing 'Moving Away From The Pulse beat'. I needed to slide my hand up the neck to play the intro. I was trying to miss it and the riff ended up sounding like a fucking Chinese cartoon: Plink, Plink, Plink, Plink, Plink.

Any way the Pistols were barred from Derby because they never turned up for the meeting, but the Damned did and they apparently agreed to the council's terms and went ahead with the gig. Johnny Thunders and The Heartbreakers were on the tour and they stuck with the Pistols in a show of solidarity, which was right. Malcolm considered the Damned had committed at an act of treachery so they got dropped and we were in. It added to some silly rivalries, and made what was already a bit of a tense tour that much worse. Although the press fabricated much of the so-called in-fighting between the punk bands at the time, some mud was thrown. Some journalists were very pro-Clash and a lot of them still hadn't accepted the Pistols. It was all a bit childish: "The Clash are fucking brilliant and the Pistols have peaked so move over..." The press have never been able to help themselves. I think Malcolm and Bernie Rhodes were genuinely in competition with each other because they used to be partners and they were out to outdo each other. Some of the newer bands too were out to get noticed and they'd say anything to some hack just to get a dig in. The Damned had said they were "better than the Pistols" and they'd apparently got people's backs up by bragging about getting the first punk single out. But, if the truth be known, that was more down to Stiff records being quick off the mark and paying sod all for it. If most of them bands were honest, they'd have to say they only rode on the Pistols' backs. We were happy with our association with the Pistols, but never saw ourselves as part of the overall punk movement. Well, I never did. Certainly not in the same way as bands like The Adverts, Chelsea, or Eater did, partly because of where we came from. We were as far removed from it mentally as we were geographically. I was proud to be associated with whatever was going on because I liked the attitude, which was fuck the music industry, fuck the government. The difference was we never had an agenda like the London bands, nor a Malcolm figure. We had our mates like Boon, and a guy called Pete Monks, trying to run things, and they were just like us. As much as I loved those bands, I could see they were becoming caricatures of themselves. They were funny and stylish and we never knew how they did it. I used to look at the Clash and listen to some of their political ramblings as well as some of the Pistols' and think, "Excuse me, I don't need you to influence me politically." I was already political. Being brought up with no money makes you political. I had read George Orwell's 1984 and Animal Farm. I thought the thing he was saying about dressing up as a traveller and going out into the world to see how it works was brilliant. That's why I was in a band to get away from a life of mending cars, rowing with my neighbours and having no money. We were ordinary kids on the street and we knew it. That's what we were interpreting in our writing, wry observations of life and love in the North, the only difference was we were using guitars to do it. That's not to say the Clash never gave me food for thought. Of course they did. It's just that I felt I was writing about things closer to home. It certainly wasn't all love songs. I couldn't have written a song like 'Autonomy' if I had my head up my arse. Joe Strummer said that was one of his all-time favourite songs. Our songs had a lot of social comment and were full of social circumstance. No, I didn't care about the Guatemalan rebels and I didn't think I could turn Northern Ireland around by finger-pointing. I knew life was a lot more complicated. I was more interested in why a girl might end up working her whole life on a supermarket checkout.

We never found out the full story of why the Damned were dropped but that's Malcolm all over. If he thought it made more sense to have a local band (with a following) supporting the Pistols, that's what he'd have – especially if that band had some history and even a friendship with them. The tour was designed along the lines of an old late Fifties/early Sixties revue tour, the ones where all the bands and press travel together on the same bus. By the time they'd got a quarter of the way through, The Damned were gone, most dates had been cancelled and the Clash were travelling separately. They'd had a big falling-out over the size of their billing (something that would stay with Strummer for years to come, even writing about it in 'All The Young Punks'). That was the size of things by the time we turned up. The other thing that had changed dramatically was the amount of activity surrounding the Pistols.

They were also staying at what's now the Holiday Inn. Back then it was the Midland Hotel. Top quality. We went up to their suite of rooms. When we got there, it was pandemonium. The phone was literally ringing off the hook. Malcolm was fending off people like the Daily Mirror and the Sun every five seconds. TV news stations and music papers all trying to get the lowdown. It was a crazy scene, a complete media circus all wanting to know what the Pistols were planning to do next. The Bill Grundy thing had happened and suddenly they were front-page news: "Dirty Rotten Punks", "The Filth And The Fury". Johnny was walking around drinking cough medicine out of the bottle, trying to get the opium out of it, and Steve and Paul were ordering loads of beer on room service. The waiter brought all these bottled beers up. Everyone had their feet up on this long highly polished table, which they were using to crack the tops off the bottles. The waiter was going mad saying, "No, no, no, no, you can't do that" and Steve was winding him up, "It's alright, man," and offering him a beer. Then John presented Shelley with a plate: on it was a big banana and two oranges arranged like a big dick.

The gig was fantastic. The Electric Circus had come into its own by now and a lot of the bigger bands were playing there. It had become the place to play in Manchester, this rundown old cinema, dark and seedy, just right for that night and perfect for that package. Glen said afterwards it had been the best night of the entire tour – not that there were many to choose from being as the whole thing had been whittled down to about three dates out of something like nineteen. Nevertheless, it was fantastic from our point of view. It was our turning point. It was sold out. We had a big home crowd in there rooting for us. We had come home to roost. It was a turning point for music in Manchester, too. The Stiff Kittens were apparently formed after seeing that gig (they became Joy Division). A young fan called Steven Morrissey put an ad in Sounds straight after asking for musicians to form a punk band. I remember the back stage party ended with us nailing Johnny Thunders' leather jacket to the dressing room door.

The only downer came a week later when Pete Silverton a reviewer for Sounds called us "A second-rate provincial Pistols copy." It made us wonder: was he actually there?

Some more History, 1977-style:

"No Elvis, Beatles or the Rolling Stones," the Clash sang that year. It wasn't strictly true. Sure, Keith Richards had his problems: he was charged with possessing enough heroin and cocaine that he faced trafficking charges in Toronto Canada. It was a charge that carried a life sentence if he pleaded guilty or a mere seven years if he didn't. Tricky! The Stones still managed to reach number three with their double Love You Live album, though. The Beatles went two places higher and hit the top spot with their own live outing, The Beatles At The Hollywood Bowl, selling over a million copies. Elvis? Oh, right: he died.

Following the infamous Bill Grundy Today Show incident, Punk exploded. It was no longer a secret movement presided over by a few in-the-know fashion-setters. Nor was it confined to the trendier parts of inner London or, for that matter, Manchester. Now every provincial outpost throughout the British Isles had learnt of its terror. TV sets across the land had been kicked in. Breakfast headlines warned of the imminent breakdown of society. Anarchy in the UK. The Sex Pistols had surreptitiously infiltrated England's establishment and scurrilously signed a recording deal with EMI, the bloody Beatles' label, for Christ's sake! Not that they were the first off the contractual starting blocks. That distinction belonged to those much-reviled funsters, The Damned, the alleged instigators of the near-blinding of a girl fan at the 100 Club. They'd already issued this vile fad's first bona fide punk 45rpm months ago, and teenagers everywhere were bringing it into your home. The undeniably fine single 'New Rose' had been recorded on budget of £50, and sold over 4000 copies on mail order before United Artists picked it up and distributed it nationwide. The Clash had taken their pseudo-terrorist stance and, according to Sniffin' Glue, sold it out to the mainstream (CBS) for one hundred thousand pieces of gold.

Record companies were falling over their chequebooks signing any group, new or old (for that matter, young or old), that would nail its colours firmly to the punk mast. Chancers like The Stranglers, who'd signed to United Artists on the back of their pub rock credentials, punked it up, and were selling copies of their debut album Rattus Norvegicus quicker than shellfish in a east London boozer. It was a scenario reminiscent of the Merseybeat boom of the early Sixties. Back then, in the wake of the Beatles, and indeed Dick Rowe's classic lack of judgement, all a group had to do was get some Cuban heels, a Rickenbacker guitar and a provincial accent.

That was all they needed. Now it was safety pins, spiky hair and a pair of bondage trousers: Generation X were going worldwide with Chrysalis, Slaughter and The Dogs with Decca, The Adverts with Stiff and even The Vibrators at CBS. Large numbers of music fans remained unconvinced. Unsure of punk's musical merit, they kept the likes of Rod Stewart, Elton John and Queen in the top five.

However, with the NME, Sounds and DJs like John Peel and Anne Nightingale, all flying the punk flag, the new wave drenched the nation. It seemed that groups literally formed over night and became household names by teatime. Bands like X-Ray Spex, The Undertones, Penetration, 999, The Lurkers, The Cure, Sham 69, Stiff Little Fingers and one group that would ultimately outsell them all, The Jam. All of them cropping up from provinces far and wide, market towns and villages; all adding to the sizable stable of bands formed by the scene's original movers and shakers.

# CHAPTER FIVE
# DO IT YOURSELF

ODEON HAMMERSMITH Tel. 01-748-4081
Manager: Philip Leivers
STRAIGHT MUSIC presents
BUZZCOCKS

EVENING 7-30 p.m.
Saturday, Nov. 4th, 1978

STALLS
£2·50

LOCK

22        B30

It's funny but, even though the Pistols, the Damned and even the fucking Vibrators had been signed up, I don't think it bothered us either way. We certainly weren't panicking about getting a deal. We hadn't been together long enough. We were more concerned with getting better as a band, better songs and better players. Malcolm said to us every time we saw him: "Get signed up before it's too late!" We used to laugh. We all agreed: What's the rush? We weren't aware that all these London record companies were cutting each other's throats trying to sign groups. To be honest, we were a bit in the dark as to what was going on outside of Manchester. And it was always said that A&R men didn't go beyond the Watford Gap. Anyway, what little I did see coming though, I thought was a bit cheesy. For example, the Vibrators had a single out with Chris Spedding who was one of the fucking Wombles (the one with the flying V guitar). The single was called 'Pogo Dancing' which was meant to be the punk dance. Now, I know there were some great records out in the Fifties all about dance crazes – Chubby Checker doing 'The Twist' etc – but the Pogo? The bandwagon was already overloading so to speak.

Devoto probably had his finger a little bit more on the pulse than the rest of us because he came up with the idea of starting our own label and putting our own record out. It sounds nothing now but back then it was a pretty radical thing to do. We already had the New Hormones office set up at his house so it made sense that New Hormones would also be the name of the label.

The next time we were back at Lifeline, we chose a song each. We wanted to record an EP mainly because we wanted it to come with a picture sleeve just like the old Sixties EPs. My choice was 'Breakdown'; the other three tracks were 'Time's Up', 'Friends Of Mine' and 'Boredom'. We recorded it at Indigo studios, with this strange guy called Martin Zero, better known now as Martin Hannett, who did all the Joy Division stuff. Back then, however, he worked for the Manchester Review. He told us he was really a producer and that wanted to help us out, so we let him. To be honest, I don't think he'd ever recorded anything in his life. He was an eccentric electronics boffin, who drove the studio's engineer mad.

Every time the engineer got the sound just right Martin would lean across and fuck it up. He must have done it a hundred times until the engineer gave up and let him mix it his way. That's why we ended up with that poxy tinny sound. I don't know to this day if that's what he intended to do or even if that's how he heard it. What I do know is we could never get that sound again, thank fuck.

Shelley's Dad lent us the money to record it, something like two or three hundred pounds, and Sue Cooper put in a hundred pounds out of her University fees to cover the pressing. One of Boon's mates called Dave Sowden also put some money in, which probably paid for the printing. Boon had an old black-and-white Polaroid camera, so he took the front cover shot of us standing in Piccadilly Gardens by the statue of Robert Peel. He only had two shots left in it so we had to make sure we didn't blink. We fucked the first one up but thankfully managed to keep our eyes open for the second. Devoto found some pressing plant down in London that would press up one thousand copies for five hundred pounds.

I couldn't believe it was so easy. It sounds stupid now but I couldn't get my head around the fact that we would have our own record. I kept thinking, "Surely, it won't be the same as a real one. It can't be!" When we finally got the call from the plant to say they were ready, I drove down to London with Devoto to pick them up. We pulled into this industrial estate. There in front of us was a big pallet all wrapped in cellophane with our name on. The excitement was unbelievable. We were like kids at Christmas, ripping at the wrapping, until there it was, all black, shiny and new. As I held it, slipping it in and out of its fresh white cover, I still kept thinking, "There must be something more to it than this. It can't be the same fucking product as a real record, not like the singles I buy in Woolworths."

Another myth was blown away; records weren't magic and just like songs they didn't come fully formed either. They came from an industrial estate in southwest London and you put them in the sleeves yourself.

We took them all back to Devoto's, bought some wine and sat up all night, checking each and every one for scratches and putting them in the covers. Each copy went out with a little leaflet, which said: "This is almost certainly going to be a limited edition release; there won't be much advertising". Thanks to Martin we got to use the Manchester Review's address to receive mail and send out copies.

I say we checked every copy that went out, but obviously our quality control wasn't the best because the first review we got was from Sniffin' Glue, saying: "The first time I played this thing, it jumped all over the place. So I threw it against the wall and it broke into pieces". He was kind enough to say the Buzzcocks are the new wave and also put in the address and the price, one pound plus ten pence post and packaging, a bargain.

The official release date was Saturday the 29th of January 1977. Rough Trade records picked up the distribution and, within a week we'd sold the lot, nearly a thousand copies.

It literally flew out. Rough Trade's boss Geoff Travis said in Sounds, "It was the first independent record people really wanted. We must have ordered hundreds of them." After doing the maths, we realised we needed to sell six hundred copies in order to pay everyone back. We were in profit. It was meant to have been a limited edition but it went so well we ended up pressing about twenty thousand. That's enough to keep you at number one for a month nowadays. It was going so well that the Virgin Records store in Manchester rang us to say it was their best-selling single.

John Peel played it on BBC Radio One. Melody Maker wrote: "This is fast, sparse, intense and red hot with the spirit and emotion of rock and roll." NME wrote: "'Spiral Scratch' is heavily New York-influenced in style." That inveterate letter writer, Stephen Morrissey, wrote to the same paper to say "The Buzzcocks differ in one way from their contemporaries; they possess a spark of originality!" Wooo hooo, the only way is up!

Oh, wait a minute! The lead singer's leaving!

Yes, that little bombshell dropped out of the blue. We'd just turned up at his house for a rehearsal when all of a sudden he turned around to us in his living room and calmly said, "Oh, by the way, I'm leaving."

We just looked at him totally shocked, in silence and disbelief. He went on with some crap, saying he felt he'd achieved all the things he wanted to achieve whilst being in a band – which was bollocks. What had we really done? We were only just starting to make some headway. Punk was setting the county alight and we were in the running. The whole thing was evolving before our very eyes. It was still early days. What the fuck is he on about? He made some speech about how he'd wanted to make a record and now he had, how he'd wanted to support the Pistols and he'd done that too. Now, he said, "there was nothing left to do." I just thought, "You cunt, this is the worst possible time to go."

The real reason he was going was so he could finish his college exams, which was fair enough, but to imply this thing had run its course was nonsense. He'd only played eleven gigs, for fuck's sake.

It took Shelley and me about five minutes to look at each other and say, "We'll carry on without you." It wasn't an option for either of us: we had sod all else. We both knew it would be difficult to replace a front man and lead singer with someone completely new, so we decided not to bother.

The band was still in one piece, sound-wise. After all, we still had John. I always felt that Devoto was a law unto himself anyway. He was a lot more self-contained and came from a different angle to the rest of us, his own personal angle.

At first, the loss of our singer felt like a massive gap to close but, as soon as Shelley took over the vocals, it was like a revelation. It was an amazing and crucial kick up the arse.

The whole situation was resolved in minutes.

It also opened up an opportunity for me. I said to him, if you move over to vocals, then I'll move over to guitar because I never really wanted to be the fucking bass player in the first place. I was never comfortable being the bass player. It wasn't my forte, so I said we'll put out an ad for a real one.

As it turned out, we didn't need to advertise because Shelley said he had it covered. He had a mate who would jump at the chance: Garth Davies.

We had quite a few gigs scheduled, including another punk festival, again with the Pistols and the Clash. This was going to be a much bigger event held at the Global Village in London's Charing Cross. We were up against it time-wise which made Devoto's decision to leave all the more annoying.

I was pissed off that we didn't have time to audition a bass player and a bit sceptical about having one of Shelley's pals just walk on in. Shelley knew this so he made a half-arsed attempt at advertising for a bass player by putting an ad in the Virgin Records shop window. He wrote "Leading North-West beat combo require bass player who is pretty or competent, or pretty competent."

If I was sceptical beforehand, it was nothing to how I felt the minute I clapped eyes on Garth: I thought a fucking breakdown man had turned up to tow the van away! Garth was a massive truck driver-type of a guy, a huge build of a man, a proper bruiser. He was completely and totally inappropriate for the band. I think Pete's judgement was way off on that one. I felt Pete wasn't bothered about how we looked as a band, something that really mattered to John and me. He's still a bit blind to that one! His argument was that he simply didn't want to lose any of the momentum. I suppose he did have a point. We did have commitments, plus we'd be all right if the van broke down.

Apart from Garth's girth, there was something fundamentally good about him. He had a lot of fire, a lot of anger, and that added to the group's dynamic. Unfortunately, you knew it couldn't last. He was the sort that ultimately self-destructs. It's just a matter of time. Having said that, he was also one of the best drinkers I'd ever met so I made a conscious effort to get along with him. The only trouble with that was we got on too well. We started going off on two-to three-day benders, pub-crawls and all-day boozing.

Shelley would come along to start with but he would always fall by the wayside after a couple of hours and we'd carry on into the night. We never could make it home so we got into a habit of turning up at Devoto's place, an old Victorian house converted into flats. He had a couple of rooms on the ground floor, in one of which we still used to rehearse from time to time.

It wasn't as if we were strangers… Devoto wouldn't think it too much of an imposition, surely?

The people in the other flats, on the other hand, hated the fucking sight of us. Devoto's face was always a picture: every time he'd open that door, you'd hear his heart sink. We would sleep in the back room on this rotten old settee thing that pulled out to a bed, which was fucking horrible, a real health hazard. We'd been crashing there for ages: many a time we'd have five, six or even eight people on that thing. Smelly feet and birds' smelly fannies. It was a regular occurrence: feeling some bird up while someone was shagging next to you. You'd wake up and think, "Fucking hell! I ain't doing this again." You'd be back the next night.

We'd always start off with every intention of getting home – "We'll have one more and I'll get the bus and I'll see you tomorrow" – but it never ever happened. We'd get absolutely slaughtered and realise, once again, we couldn't get home, so we'd go and knock on his door again. Three or four nights in a row this would happen. This was the routine: meet in the pub at twelve, no breakfast, drink until they closed at half past three, go to the off licence, buy enough booze to see us though the afternoon, back in there at five. This would go on for days. We'd even go to the Electric Circus, which was nowhere near Devoto's house, and we'd still find our way back there.

In the end, he had to put a stop to it because the people in the other flats were going to get him thrown out. At one point he begged us to stop coming back. He was very polite about it and said his neighbours "were a bit disgruntled with us" so we said: "Alright, Howard, this will be the last time."

Sure enough, the next day we did the round of pubs, went to the Electric Circus and broke in though Devoto's kitchen window.

Garth wasn't only good for getting drunk with. He made a big difference to the band. He freed us up and made it possible to move on to the next phase. I was a lot happier on guitar and suddenly everything was a lot more accessible. I was always a bit inhibited by Devoto's artsy-fartsy antics so I liked Garth's street-level approach. We suddenly sounded like we had some bollocks.

By the way, the Global Village gig never happened after all. The first time we played live with Garth was supporting the Clash at the Harlesden Coliseum in London. The Slits were playing their first gig and it was our second time in London. We knew it was an important gig for us: Devoto was gone, we had a juggernaut on bass and we were going to follow a group of girls who, by all accounts, wear underpants over their tights and get their tits out. We were determined to make a big impression. The Clash were really taking off at this point: they had an album out and were wearing their painted-up military-styled clobber with all the zips. They were looking a million dollars.

Not to be outdone, we wore screen-printed shirts based on a Piet Mondrian design made by a friend of Boon's called Janey Collings – well, Garth didn't. We put him in a boiler suit. And I say screen-printed: well, they weren't, they were hand-painted – and they left the exact same pattern on our chests when we took them off. We were literally covered in hundreds of little yellow, black, and red squares all over our bodies. It looked like a fucking tattoo.

That aside, the Coliseum was without a doubt our best performance to date. As a result, we were offered the support on the Clash's first major UK tour.

We did a few warm-ups leading up to the White Riot tour, one in Brighton and another in London at the Roxy. That was the night a busload of Buzzcocks fans actually travelled down from Manchester, another first.

Shelley was so touched he went back in the bus with them but somehow got left behind, after falling asleep at Scratchwood Services.

We did another show supporting Manchester's very own Sad Café. They were doing a one-off show at Blackburn's Golden Palms.

When we arrived for the soundcheck, all their gear was already set up, fucking tons of it: bongos, percussion, keyboards and, of course, the gong. We walked on the stage and asked one of their endless roadies where they wanted us to set up."Down there," we were told. They actually expected us to play on the floor in front of the stage. Rather than move a single flugelhorn, we would have to play in the audience.

So that's what we did, played our set with the entire crowd standing about two feet in front of us. It could have been soul-destroying if it wasn't for roughly half the crowd leaving once we'd finished.

We held court with most of them in a pub around the corner afterwards. I snuck back to see the sad Sad Café playing to a half-empty hall.

We also made our first TV appearance in the lead up to the Clash tour. Tony Wilson had a 'Yoof' TV programme called What's On broadcast by

Granada. We were asked to do it, representing the Sound of Young Manchester. Albert Finney was on plugging some play and talking about being a Salford lad. They also had a big eagle on that shat all over him. We were booked to do one number 'Boredom'. So we did that, met Albert Finney and Shelley got his dole stopped. Apparently, someone at his unemployment office saw the show and recognised him. He lost his tenner a week. Fame at last.

The White Riot tour opened on Sunday the first of May 1977 at Guildford's Civic Hall.

The initial line-up was The Clash, the Jam and the Buzzcocks, plus some other smaller bands in different parts of the country. Subway Sect was on some dates. So were the Slits and a band called the Prefects. It was obviously based on the Pistols' "Anarchy" tour but, because that one had been such a fiasco with so many dates cancelled, this was really the country's first proper punk tour. It was a fucking good package for two pounds-twenty a ticket, that's for sure.

On the first night, I remember walking through the backstage area at soundcheck and hearing the opening lines of 'This is the Modern World'. I didn't know who was playing it but I thought, "Fuck, that's a tasty song!" I pushed though the curtains surrounding the stage and there was the Jam.

I hadn't met them before but I had their first album In The City and I thought, "That's cool: that song's not on it."

They were visually unique and very striking. I still considered myself to be a bit of a mod (or at least a monk – © John Lennon) so I identified with their image straightaway. It was during their black-suit period: they had the black-and-white shoes, the red Rickenbackers and the Union Jacks. All very Who, of course.

Weller had a reputation of being an arrogant and moody bastard and, on the whole, he didn't disappoint. Saying that, I always felt he was shy more than anything else.

We never really got further than nodding acquaintance, even though our dressing room ended up next to theirs on more than one occasion. On this particular night, for example, they were like two little toilets next to one another. I'll never forget watching their roadies wheel in three fucking flight cases just for their clothes. I couldn't believe it! Each one had their names stencilled on the side: Paul, Rick, and Bruce. All their gear was hung up in them with little drawers for their socks and shoes. I thought, "Fucking Hell! In a place like this, that's a bit unnecessary!" It was bloody impressive, though.

It was early days for them and that was fucking slick. I was still getting my pinstriped suits from Oxfam. They were two or three years younger than us – and they looked it. They seemed very childlike but you knew they meant business because of those flight cases. Everyone else was into this or that type of amp or guitar but I couldn't get over those fucking flight cases!

The Jam left a good impression on me even though they were very cool to us. Then again, every group was a bit self-contained at that point. There certainly wasn't the sort of banter we'd had with the Pistols. People were friendly but there was an overall feeling of tension and frustration among the groups. It didn't bother me because I felt it helped everyone's performances each night: every band would really explode on stage. It was as if each band had something to prove and they didn't want to give anything away. They were all saving it all for their gig.

Quite a few people didn't get along with Weller. He had recently made some pro-Tory comment which hadn't gone down particularly well in the Clash camp. He'd also allegedly bottled Sid Vicious in the 100 Club and burnt a copy of Sniffin' Glue live on stage. He was making a bit of a name for himself.

He wanted to be seen as tough but he wasn't scary at all – coming out of the Electric Circus onto the Council estate: that was scary. I could tell he had the angst and the bitterness, though! He had Woking grit to work out of his system. He'd read George Orwell and he felt the British constitution was open to question. Fair enough but he ended up coming across like some comprehensive school kid wanting to make a point. He had that simple comprehensive school mentality. He didn't have an overview. The Clash seemed to have a broader outlook. In political terms, Weller wanted to be a Beatle.

That was a good call as far as I was concerned, but it seemed at odds with what the Clash were all about. They were singing about prostitutes and Sten guns in fucking Knightsbridge! The first couple of nights went fantastic but I could tell all was not well in the Jam camp: Weller was very moody, keeping himself to himself, smoking and spitting a lot. There was, apparently, a bust-up over money – and lots of accusations of sound-tampering. I don't know the whole story but whatever happened was enough for them to quit the tour after a couple of gigs. We moved up a rung.

I don't blame them for doing the off because they didn't really fit in. I'm sure Weller saw the Jam as a headliner band and wasn't comfortable playing second fiddle to anyone, especially to a Clash audience. He had a point: the Jam were making a lot of headway at that time. Pretty soon, they'd be selling out the same venues under their own name.

I never found out the full story but it had obviously rubbed Strummer up the wrong way, just as his gripe with the Pistols had. Once again, he committed it to song: he wrote a little dig at the Jam into the Clash single 'White Man in Hammersmith Palais', sneering: "The new groups are not concerned with what there is to be learned/they wear Burton suits and think it's funny turning rebellion into money."

Make of that what you will.

We were happy just getting on with it and giving the Clash a run for their money. We made a massive impact on that tour and the Clash respected us for it. They loved having these Mancunian guys around. We were their poor relations, but we were really gave it one hundred and ten per cent each night.

One night Strummer's guitar packed up and he asked to borrow mine. I didn't watch the Clash that night so I left it with him. That was a mistake because I got it back the following night in a right state: he'd cut up a newspaper and stuck it all over it. Big fucking newsprint headlines covered in glue: "Strike Action" or some such bollocks and one machine head broken off. I was so pissed off I wanted to punch his face in. It was the best guitar I had, plus we were due on in ten minutes. I barged into their dressing room. Strummer turned round and – lo and behold! – pulled a machine head out of his pocket. Guitarists just don't carry machine heads around, so he must have known why I was fuming.

The trouble with Strummer was that he was such a likeable bloke, it was hard to keep angry with him. He completely softened the blow. He handed it to me and said maybe this one will fit? It was a horrible little plastic one off of a cheap acoustic guitar, which I had to fiddle around with just before I went on. It looked so shit stuck on the end and the glue made the fucking thing really sticky. I was standing on the stage thinking, "How the fuck did he get away with this?" I still have that guitar, and now I think it's great but at the time I thought, "That fucking Strummer dissed my guitar!"

That tour was another turning point, certainly a factor in landing us our deal with United Artists. Unfortunately, it was also the beginning of the end for Garth. We were all drinking massive amounts on the road but Garth was way ahead of everyone, his intake was off the scale. One big nail in his coffin was hammered in at an aftershow party at the Clash's hotel. It was a really hip party. All the press had been invited and there was a lot of sucking up going down. Garth somehow managed to get into a fight with one of the bouncers and ended up calling him a cunt.

All hell broke lose. Garth ended up rolling around the floor fighting six of them, tables were going over and glasses were smashing. It was really heavy. Finally, they got the better of him. All six bouncers lifted him up by his arms and legs and ran him though the door headfirst.

Change to Strummer and Mick Jones would still talk about this 20 years later. They couldn't believe it: all four of them, dressed up like fucking SAS storm troopers, just standing there, freaked out.

I couldn't help laugh. The Clash were supposed to be this really hard and confrontational band because they'd just come back from Northern Ireland where they had their pictures taken standing by the barbed wire and all that. Yet the sight of Garth picking up chairs and trying to smash them over a bouncer's head was a bit too real. There was nothing glamorous about it, that's for sure. Garth looked like a fat clumsy droog from Clockwork Orange, all boiler suit and boots being carried out, kicking and screaming.

It was a shame and it ruined the atmosphere somewhat. At the same time, it was also symbolic of his exit from the Buzzcocks. The Clash remember it because, if anyone wasn't taking any shit from society, it was Garth.

There was a review I read somewhere of that night's gig where someone wrote: "Garth looks like he could take on a room full of Teddy Boys with one hand behind his back." Insightful.

As the doors swung shut behind them, all eyes turned to us.

It was time for a show of Northern solidarity. We finished our beers and left as discreetly as possible, crunching over the broken glass.

As I feared, Garth had disappeared into the night streets of Leicester or Nottingham or wherever we were. This could be bad because we knew he could quite easily disappear for days on end.

We must have walked around for hours before Shelley decided he'd had enough and called the police saying, "We're looking for a great big bloke dressed in a boiler suit and covered in blood." We eventually caught up with him down some side street miles away from the hotel, still pissed out of his head. As we got close to him, you could tell he was crazed and on something or other as soon as he saw us he turned and started shouting, "Don't come fucking near me or I'll kill you." I thought, "That's fucking gratitude. I've just left a party full of free booze to find you."

It was like talking down a sucide. We tried everything, saying, "Come on, Garth! We've got a gig tomorrow: come back with us" and "You've got to come back with us, Garth. We need you," but all he would say was "Keep your fucking distance."

After two hours of that I was ready to leave him where he was. I thought, "It's four o'clock in the fucking morning and it's bad enough doing this tour without all this shit." Just then he seemed to snap out of it and said, "Okay then, I'll come back. I'll just have a piss around the corner and I'll come back."

He walked off and I said to Shelley "Thank fuck for that!" Ten minutes later, I looked at Shelley again and said, "It doesn't take that long to piss." We peered around the corner. Sure enough, he'd disappeared again.

The police eventually picked him up and retuned him to us.

We were all staying in one room in a B&B, all lined up like sardines, when all these coppers brought him in. We had to be up in about an hour. All he could say was "No one says a fucking word." I could think of two: you're sacked.

However, that wasn't quite the end of Garth. He lived to fight another day. The next time was Leeds. Shelley went onstage wearing a Manchester United football top. He wasn't trying to be provocative. It was just a shirt to him. He wasn't stylish enough to wear something provocative. I tried to explain to him it probably wasn't a good idea but he wouldn't listen.

We got though about two numbers before the first pint glass hit the stage. Someone spat at Shelley and Garth offered the entire audience out. Garth waded into the front row as the entire stage was pelted with bottles and glasses.

I tried to defuse the situation by playing the opening few bars of the nation's current number one favourite, 'Angelo' by The Brotherhood of Man, but do you know what? It only seemed to make matters worse.

We had to make a quick exit so we made a mad dash for the car we'd hired. We were chased outside by about a hundred blokes and only managed to scramble into the car before the back window was put though by a house brick.

The crowd completely surrounded us and Garth was trying to get out. One guy was banging on the window and, like an idiot, Garth rolled it down and got smashed in the face. There was blood pouring out of his nose and the crowd were kicking the car to pieces, smashing the lights and mirrors.

We somehow managed to pull away. I remember John was busting for a piss but there was no way we were stopping until we'd put a good couple of miles between us. Eventually, he couldn't wait any longer and screamed at Boon to stop the car. As he started to slow down, John swung the door open and the fucking thing hit a lamppost and came away from its hinges. When we got home, the car looked like it'd been in a stock car race, the back seat was covered in blood and glass and the door was completely fucked. We parked it on the hire car forecourt before they opened and legged it.

CHAPTER SIX
# WHAT DO
## WE GET?

ODEON HAMMERSMITH Tel. 01-748-4081
Manager: Philip Leivers
STRAIGHT MUSIC presents
BUZZCOCKS
EVENING 7-30 p.m.
Saturday, Nov. 4th, 1978
STALLS
£2·50
BLOCK

22 / R30

73

Our relationship with Garth really started to deteriorate during that summer of 1977. His behaviour had got crazier and crazier and his unpredictability (never a good quality) had started to become a liability. He was now inciting trouble and picking fights over the most ridiculous things. Once he tried to beat Shelley up because he'd bought the wrong size batteries for his ghetto blaster. He also started to rant and rave at the crowd and walk off mid-number. We all persevered with him though and he was still a Buzzcock at the time we signed our record deal.

Andrew Lauder was the guy who eventually signed us up to United Artists. He'd been up to Manchester and saw us play the Electric Circus supported by Joy Division. It was one of their first gigs. They weren't even called Joy Division then: they were called Warsaw. Crap name, but better than the Stiff Kittens, which was the name Shelley gave them.

Lauder was a nice guy. I remember him shitting hisself that night because his hotel was miles away and he didn't want to walk back though the council estate on his own afterwards.

He made a really big play for us and said in the press he'd made up his mind to sign us without even seeing us. Which was a load of bollocks because he came to a lot of gigs before he actually got the chequebook out. We'd suddenly become hot property since doing the White Riot tour. Every major label was after us and Boon was taking up to six to seven calls a day. CBS, and EMI were ringing constantly but we decided to hold out because we didn't want to get caught in a situation where we sign up and then find out we could or couldn't do such and such a thing. The Clash had told us that they were already having problems with CBS. They were singing about complete control, or rather the lack of it, and threatening all sorts of legal shit. We didn't want to fall into the same trap. We spent quite a few drunken nights out on Lauder's expense account and he came across as a good guy, a real music enthusiast. He said all the right things: we could have total artist control, we could put whatever single out and have whatever we liked on the sleeve. That swayed it for us. We all thought this is a much better bet than going with one of the majors. He seemed to have full empathy with the band and understand exactly what we were trying to do, even if we didn't.

CBS got really pissed off with us. The head guy there at the time, Maurice Oberstein, was going, "You guys are crazy. You could have an open cheque book here. You can have as much money as you want if you sign to CBS."

The Clash situation put us off CBS because we knew we'd encounter the same bureaucratic bullshit they were fighting.

So we opted for Lauder and his promise of a free rein. There's a famous picture of us with him, all blind drunk after our gig, signing the contracts on the bar of the Electric Circus. It was bizarre because Elvis had died that morning, Tuesday the 16th of August, and all the punks at the gig were cheering and saying, "Good job, the fat cunt".

We got something like seventy-five grand advance for the first two years, which Oberstein said he would top.

To give him his due, he was ringing Boon right to the bitter end, saying: "You are mad to sign to Lauder. Don't do it. You'll regret it." Nevertheless despite the temptation of a lot more money, we all agreed that we'd made the right choice. To be fair to Lauder, he was started off as good as his word. He let us have the freedom he'd promised so we released 'Orgasm Addict' as our first single. Lo and behold, United Artists refuse to press the fucking thing! The press department refused to work on it too because it had "orgasm" in the title which they thought was disgusting. That delayed everything for a couple of months. No sooner had we sorted that one out, the second single was due: 'What Do I Get?' with 'Oh Shit' on the B-side. The same thing happened again, only this time it was worse: this time the staff actually walked out. Lauder spent most of his time trying to pacify and appease everyone, assuring the staff that United Artists hadn't degenerated and slunk into this void of filth.

We had a clause in our contract which stated a proportion of our advance must be used to buy new equipment, something that was well overdue. We went out and bought our own P.A. system, a mixing desk, new drums and guitars. Shelley bought his first Gordon Smith Gypsy, Garth got a Gibson Thunderbird and I bought a yellow Gibson junior from Orange on Shaftesbury Avenue. It was a beautiful guitar, a 1959 model, with just two switches, volume and tone. Mick Jones had a red one. This one had belonged to Tony Hicks out of the Hollies. I thought that was pretty cool because he was from Manchester too.

The first time I used it was at Olympic Studios a few days later. I swear I'd only had it out of its case for about a minute when none other than Tony fucking Hicks himself popped his head round the door. He clocked the guitar instantly and shouted, "Oy, that's my fucking guitar!" I thought, "Fucking hell, it's been nicked!" I told him I'd just bought it from Orange, as this huge wave of guilt washed over me. He came strolling over and flipped it over to check. There was no need to because it was undoubtedly his, the cunt in the shop had told me so.

It was very unnerving because he looked so serious. He started saying, "Yeh, yeh, yeh, it's definitely my guitar," He plugged it in and started to play it. All the time I'm thinking, "Fucking hell, I'll have to give the thing back now!" Thankfully, after a few minutes he said, "I've no idea why I ever sold this." Phew!

I went on, somewhat pathetically, "Well, it's gone into good hands, Tone, because we're the Buzzcocks and we're from Manchester, too. I'm taking this guitar on to the next phase." It's funny I used that guitar on every single we made, right up to the split. It got stolen at the very first rehearsal I did afterwards. I left it in my car while I went to the pub. Big mistake.

Now that we had a label and a bit of money behind us, the visual aspect of the band was something else that really started to take shape. Devoto had saddled us with an arty tag, so we worked on developing that side of the things. Malcolm Garrett, who I think was a friend of Boon's, came into the picture around this time. He was doing a degree of some sort at Manchester University and he came to see us and show us his portfolio.

He initially wanted to do some stuff for the band for inclusion in his course work. That sort of thing was happening a lot. Suddenly people realised they could do all sorts of things. Thanks to punk so many professions had been demystified; for example, we'd done 'Spiral Scratch' with just a Polaroid. Suddenly, people were becoming photographers and graphic designers. The guy who once wrote on the toilet wall? He's now a writer. Et cetera. They were seeing through the bullshit at last and the professional angle was going out the window.

Garrett was one of those people, him and Janey Collings, the girl who designed the two-tone green 'What Do I Get?' shirts. She was another one. She became a clothes designer because she had that punk attitude. She realised she didn't have to go to London and meet the professionals. Hers was a case of 'I'll do it myself right here, right now'. She knew she could be a part of it all. We moved into an office at 50 Newton Street straight after we signed our deal. People soon found out where we were – mainly due to the fact we spent a good proportion of every day in the Crown and Anchor pub opposite. All of a sudden, people were coming up and showing us stuff, saying, "This is what I do: are you interested?" Garrett was one of those. I have to give him credit because he spotted an open market.

You have to remember that, until punk came along, British single releases very rarely came in picture bags. As soon as punk happened, every single record did.

Except for maybe Slaughter and The Dogs. They signed to Decca Records who thought they were part of the British aristocracy and therefore the only label that refused to toe the line. They went bust within four years whilst run by Jonathan King.

Basically, a whole new industry opened up, created by and catered to by a whole new breed of artist, the record sleeve designer. Garrett came up with the famous Buzzcocks logo and I suppose he set the trend for most of our visuals.

Not that we didn't have ideas of our own. Boon had a big hand in the theme that ran though all the artwork.

To be honest, I've got to admit we became no different from the Pistols in the respect that we were stylized, artwork-wise, in much the same way they were.

They had their Jamie Reids and the London art school set and we had ours. We certainly had a highly distinctive look about everything we put out. It was all meant to refer to Pop or fine art. The Clash had their Pollock thing going and we had the Mondrian, which I thought was more abrasive art, heavy ghetto stuff that came from New York. We also had touches of Warhol, Kasimir Malevich, John Heartfield. Of course, we threw in some

Beatles for good measure. Their influence was particularly obvious on the Love Bites album where we used embossed lettering out of a white background.

As I said, we all had our own ideas. I, for one, never saw eye to eye with Garrett. My brother who had been a professional artist for years had already turned me on to so much. He would take me to art galleries all the time so I knew all about Hockney and abstract art and concept fucking art.

So suddenly we meet this guy who's still at art school who thinks he can lecture us about art while trying to persuade us to have a fucking cabbage on the our first album's front cover! He'd come up with this montage thing with eyes and teeth stuck on a cabbage head. Call me unimaginative but excuse me! I thought, "Hang on a minute! I've heard these songs and I know what sort of people played them and I don't think a fucking cabbage quite represents what we're all about." A lot of what he wanted to do was simply a billboard for his artwork. It had fuck all to do with the Buzzcocks.

A lot of it looked like childish crap if you ask me. You've only got to look at some of those Seventies concept albums where there's a fucking spaceman under water or shit like that and they look so dated. I wanted our faces on the covers.

The thing about a face is it shows a person in a place and a time. The Beatles always had their pictures on their sleeves, as did Bowie and Dylan. It showed where they were and how they looked at such and such a time. Not once did any of them have a cabbage. We'd already had a woman with an iron on her head on the front of 'Orgasm Addict'. That was meant to be art. It was supposed to represent the dehumanising of women: the statement being; that women are treated as objects and therefore no different from an iron.

I let that one go because I thought, "Well, I've used women like that so I can see where he's going." However, when it came to the first album, I thought, "I want to see the faces of the guilty parties."

I stayed up until six o'clock battling it out with Garrett over that one. He was good at colour schemes, though: the silver and the orange and all that. Then again, they're good at that on those painting-and-decorating programmes.

Unfortunately, John was the only one who agreed with me. Shelley was lightweight, blinded by the so-called science of art. Because the politics surrounding the band meant we were a democracy, I just got bored. I even got to like the two-colour seven inch sleeves he did: the pink and blue, then the brown and cream. They never looked much individually but, when viewed as a series, they worked well. He used the same two-colour theme years later when he did the sleeves for The Smiths. If you've hit on a winning formula, flog it to death.

Anyway, I didn't want to get into the realms of pretention so, in the end, I simply said: "Do it your way" – except when it came to that fucking cabbage! I fought all the way on that one. After all, there's art and there's art.

On top of all the problems we'd ran into getting our actual singles released was the ongoing problem we had with Garth. Needless to say, his behaviour and his drinking hadn't improved one bit, especially as he now had his share of our advance to fuel it.

Although any one of us could full foul of his outbursts at any given time, he was mostly on Shelley's case. He would blow up at him for the slightest of reasons and even bring up old feuds dating back to when they were at school together. He'd thrown his new Gibson bass down a flight of stairs at Olympic studios after one such argument. Another particularly bad episode happened on the way to a gig in Coventry: we went round to pick him up from his house to find he wasn't in. We found out he was down the pub so we headed off to get him and saw him walking up the street, completely pissed and carrying loads of cans. We got him in the car and he started having a go at Shelley again: Shelley had said something and Garth went berserk.

We were doing about ninety miles an hour down the motorway and the pair start fighting across the front and back seat.

Garth was shouting he was going to kill Shelley and trying to get at him so we eventually had to stop the car. Garth leapt out, still shouting at Shelley and banging on the windows, screaming at him to get out. Understandably, Shelley wasn't having any of it. We were all trying to pacify

Garth, saying, "Get back in", but he was out of control.

We finally managed to get to the gig with Shelley still in one piece. In the opening number, Garth started ranting and raving again, shouting abuse. Then he threw his bass into the amps and stormed off. I turned the bass control up on my guitar and carried on with out him. That pissed him off all the more: he stomped back onstage three songs later and started to have another rant. He picked up his bass and we started another song – only for him to repeat his performance midway though, storming off for the remainder of the set.

The atmosphere in the car on the way home was full of bad vibes. No one said a word the whole drive back to Manchester.

The writing was on the wall. I wasn't prepared to carry on like that. Luckily enough, neither was the others. We all agreed that Garth was out of control. He had to go. It fell to me to tell him he was sacked. He seemed genuinely sorry. He rang me a few days later and said he'd been to a doctor and was getting help. Too late: we were already auditioning for his replacement. To be honest, I always knew he wasn't right for the band, not least image-wise; then again, maybe he was.

The NME reported it thus: "Buzzcocks have sacked their bass player Garth Davies due to 'personal and professional incompatibility.'"

Auditions were held at a place called Drum Studios where all the Manchester bands have recorded. We had obviously made a bit of a name for ourselves by now so there was no shortage of interest. We must have tried out twenty or thirty bass players on the first day alone. It was a nightmare. Nobody worked, none of them was right. They were all musicians' musicians. None of them were happening. After about five hours of that, the three of us hid out in one of the toilet cubicles. We racked out a couple of lines of coke each (our tastes were becoming expensive) in order to get though the last two hopefuls. Suddenly, there was a knock on the door.

It seemed one guy was couldn't wait any longer and was very eager to show us exactly what he could do. He had a bass guitar strapped on so high his chin almost rested on it. We all trooped back to the rehearsal room and plugged in. I'll tell you, this guy was off the fucking wall. His thing was to walk right up to you and play his absurdly high-strung bass right in your face. He was like a mad grinning Killroy cartoon with just a head peering over the top off his guitar. You just wanted to punch him.

That was the last straw. We left the last guy playing on his own and retreated back to our cubicle.

The next day another twenty-odd people showed up and the nightmare resumed. The thing with Shelley, John and me was we'd become very intuitive and perceptive with each other. Most bands are the same: you can see though a lot of things collectively. You find you're in tune with one another, on each other's wavelength. Without speaking a word, you instinctively know when someone or something is wrong or right for the group. So far none of the people we'd seen were right. We didn't need to discuss it: they simply weren't Buzzcocks material.

One guy even expected us to learn his songs.

This went on for quite some time until one day we got down to the very last two again before we cracked up and went for the coke. We were fucked off by now because we had some gigs lined up, warm-ups for our first major UK tour. We'd had our single delayed, and word of Garth's departure was already in the press. We knew we couldn't afford another setback at such a crucial time. However, it was looking increasingly like we'd have to pull out.

Thinking about it, we did actually cancel one or two gigs including the tour's opening night, which didn't please the promoter. All of which added to the pressure to find someone. We'd had such a massive build-up for both the single and the tour and now both were being put on hold.

The romantic in me has always felt that a little bit of magic should happen the day you find the right person to play with in a band. I know I'd felt it the day I joined. Because it wasn't happening now, I suppose I was getting pretty disheartened – especially after auditioning so many players and having them all turn out non-starters.

We were at the point of considering postponing the entire tour if the last two applicants turned out to be duds. The last two up that day were a guy called Carl Mogg, who played in a Manchester band called The Smirks, and Steve Garvey. Steve was a kid from Prestwich who'd apparently seen us live quite a few times. He was friendly with The Fall and it was Martin Bramah who told him to come down and audition.

We were like: "Fucking hell, here's another two! Let's get on with it." Not very encouraging.

As luck would have it, they were both really good, well as good as each other anyway. That took us by surprise because we'd become so hacked off. All of a sudden, we went from having no one to choose from to having two. I said to Shelley, "Fuck it, they're both good at what they do. Let's take one of them because, personally, I can't audition any more." Shelley was as pissed off as I was so we adjourned to the cubicle to deliberate over another couple of lines who got the job.

In the meantime, Steve had gone with John to the sweet shop along the road to get a can of coke or something. When he came back a while later, we asked him who out of the two candidates he wanted in? Bearing in mind it was important that John felt comfortable with whoever got the gig because, after all, he was the other half of the rhythm section. He said he agreed with us and thought both players fitted in really well. He also said that while he was down the sweet shop Steve had bought him a Mars Bar. "Let's have him," he said, "He bought me a Mars." So Steve was in. It could easily have gone either way – especially when Steve told me later that he'd originally intended turning up for the audition wearing bondage trousers and a biker's jacket. Luckily, Bramah had talked him out of it and took him to an Oxfam Shop and told him to buy a thin-lapelled suit jacket and shirt. Secondhand tat, he must have thought, was more our style.

Funnily enough, I met the other guy years later and he asked me how come he didn't get the job over Steve. When I told him a Mars bar had swayed the balance, he couldn't believe it. He said, "I've wondered for twenty years why I didn't get that gig. It was all down to a sodding Mars bar? I hate sodding Mars bars."

Fortunately, Steve turned out to be the final piece of the Buzzcocks jigsaw. Unfortunately, he wasn't able to drop everything at a moment's notice and fuck off with us. We didn't especially want to cancel any more gigs and our tour was supposedly already underway.

Confident that we'd found the right man, we decided to do the next few gigs using a stand-in bass player. Steve could join officially as soon as he could. The trouble with that plan was who the fuck could we get to fill in? Hadn't we just auditioned every bass player in Manchester?

It just so happened that Devoto had finished his exams and was feeling secure enough to make another foray into the music business. He'd recently formed Magazine who'd played their debut gig supporting us, predictably enough, at the closure of the Electric Circus the previous month. They only had about three songs but they had a bass player called Barry Adamson.

He'll do, we thought. We'll nick him for a few days. It will give ole Devoto a chance to write a few more numbers.

By now, we'd missed the second date of the tour so we took up the slack on the third night in Scotland. We did all of the Scottish dates with Adamson, about four gigs. They were good shows and he did a great job but, fucking hell, you'd think he was with us for years to hear him talk about it now.

I have a vivid memory of those Scottish dates because I caught a really bad cold and sore throat on the way up there (nothing to do with snorting coke all week). I remember getting drunk on Jack and coke and getting a fried haggis from a chip shop, which I ate while drinking TCP out of the bottle.

Steve finally joined the tour and the band in Nottingham.

His first gig was at a club called Katie's, which turned out fantastic. He added a completely new dimension, not only to the sound but also the look of the band. He completed what I call the classic Buzzcocks line-up. He was very good looking and he worked hard on his image. I was impressed with him because he'd obviously done his homework musically as well. Straightaway, he complemented the songs and came up with some superb bass lines. He also pulled in the birds: as soon as he joined, I began noticing more and more girls in the audience. Strangely enough, something we never had while Garth was with us. I'm not taking anything away from the others: John was a good-looking bloke too but he was stuck at the back. Shelley obviously appealed too but it was Steve who did us the power of good.

The band suddenly had a much broader appeal. I felt we could pull in four different directions.

He couldn't be called Steve, though! There was already one of those. I soon got fed up with us both answering to it. I told him he must choose another name and he said, "People have always called me Paddy." That's what he became known as, Steve Paddy Garvey. The press release for him read: "He used to work in a musical instrument shop, but now he's blowing his own trumpet." He actually used to prepare brass, but it never mentioned that so it ended up sounding shit.

Eventually 'Orgasm Addict' came out as our first official single on United Artists. The record label took out half-page ads in all the music papers, saying, "Sorry, it took so long coming" – their first case of blatant double entendre. The press reaction to it was mixed, ranging from lukewarm to jubilant.

But we got an indication that they were following our progress with interest. The NME, for example, noted that the songs were written while Devoto was still in the band: "I sympathise with lyricist Howard Devoto's decision to leave this group because no one can hear his words. He wrote this song and the words are inaudible beyond the title refrain, which considering its inanity may or may not be a good thing."

Obviously ole Howard's keen observations of life in a baker's shop just simply passed them by. They went on to say, "It's not great, not more than mediocre, but compulsive and frantic enough." So did they like it or not? Sounds called it "One of the sharpest records ever to emerge." Record Mirror sounded almost relieved Garth had been sacked (he was pictured on the back sleeve) when they wrote, "Among the celebrations with this release comes the news bassist Garth has been fired just before they started their UK tour." The one thing they were all unanimous about was the question: will it ever get played on the radio? Of course not: the fucking thing was universally banned.

It had Shelley singing about wanking, faking an orgasm, and a picture of a naked woman with teeth for nipples and a Morphy Richards on her head on the sleeve.

Despite our radio ban, the tour was an unqualified success. We finished it on a high: we played two sold-out nights at the Marquee in London's Wardour Street. On both nights, we broke our own house attendance and we got our first full-page front-cover story in the NME.

Another first: what a great feeling that was! Finally seeing the band on that made me feel we were firmly on the map. It meant a lot to me because, in the weeks running up to it, both the Clash and the Pistols had been on the front. Now it was our turn. Fucking hell, Mick Jones was now coming to our gigs!

We'd stopped off at a service station and had our photo taken standing on the bridge that crossed the motorway and that's what they used. As I remember the blurb was positive too, talking about how we meant business and were now a force to be reckoned with. What's more, there was no comparisons made to either the Pistols or the Clash.

We had our own identity at last.

With our pressing plant and line-up problems safely behind us, the singles started to flow, five in a row and in practically as many months.

It's Punk but not as we know it.

Way back in 1976, Mark Perry, Sniffin' Glue's creator and main scribe, famously wrote "Give up your job, don't pay tax, and form a group." By 1978, he'd done at least two of those things. He'd folded Sniffin' Glue at the end of 1977 after twelve insightful issues and formed the experimental ATV. Punk had quite simply become far too mainstream to justify its very own underground journal. Not that Sniffin' Glue itself was that underground any more: the last issue had sold in its thousands.

Perry had developed a strong distaste for a movement that had gone decidedly off. Within the pages of those dozen issues, the whole scene had been summed up, from start to finish. For twelve glorious months, they'd chronicled and championed some of the most important music of the decade. Unfortunately, they'd also watched as the movement (which they had done so much to inspire) went from optimism and determination though rejection to acceptance and onto dissipation. By 1978, it had started to dissolve, the flame was going out. Sure, punk had given music in general the much-needed kick up the arse. It had also brought back the importance of the seven-inch single but, as the New Year dawned, it was becoming obvious that punk was failing to live up to its original promise. The Pistols had shot themselves firmly in the foot by sacking bass player (and chief songwriter) Glen Matlock. They'd replaced him with the gormless and musically inept Sid Vicious, toured America and split up. The Dammed, down to two original members, announced they had outlived their usefulness and split up, too.

So did Johnny Thunders and the Heartbreakers, along with Slaughter and the Dogs, the Vibrators and Eater. Longevity, it seemed, wasn't punk's strong point. In little over a year, the whole scene had totally fragmented and divided. Then it divided again, and subdivided even further. It was now called new wave music, a poppy mishmash of styles, skinny ties and sneakers.

It gave rise to the cod rock-reggae of bleached blond boffins the Police; the clumsy and gummy chorus-line knees-up that was the Skids; the dark gothic and downright depressing Joy Division; and Belfast's own orphans, The Undertones. Throw in the poor man's Mick Jagger, Bob Geldof, Gay Lib spokesperson Tom Robinson, and even Howard Devoto's arty sixth form creation Magazine and you have every punk crossover imaginable.

There was also Powerpop, led by ex-Pistol Glen Matlock's Rich Kids, The Pleasers, the Jags and Tonight; the first stirrings of the Mod revival, Ska and Rockabilly. Johnny Rotten reverted to plain John Lydon and formed the industrial PIL. From out of nowhere, a skinhead revival violently attached itself to the careers of well-meaning innocents like Jimmy Pursey's Sham 69.

Against this diverse musical background, the Buzzcocks prepared to release their debut long player.

CHAPTER SEVEN
# OLYMPIC STUDIO
## TO KITCHEN
### QUEEN

ODEON HAMMERSMITH Tel. 01-748-4081
Manager: Philip Leivers
STRAIGHT MUSIC presents
BUZZCOCKS

EVENING 7-30 p.m.
Saturday, Nov. 4th, 1978

STALLS
£2·50

LOCK

22 / R30

We started recording the album at Olympic studios in Barnes, which was fantastic. I knew all the great bands had recorded there: the Who, the Stones and even the Beatles. The minute I walked in the place I thought of that famous semi-coherent art flick made by Jean-Luc Godard, One Plus One. The segments showing the Stones recording 'Sympathy For The Devil' were all filmed in there: Brian Jones is out of it and they're all doing the Woo-woohs around the mike. Those sound screens that the Stones are using were still there when we were in. The room looked exactly the same.

It was like an old school hall, a massive big orchestra-sized room. We had our little amps set up right in the middle of it. You could feel the ghosts in there and I'm convinced a bit of magic dust rubbed off because we were treading a well-worn path. It had a brilliant feel for recording. We had just bought these flanges because we were using these poxy little H+H amps which everybody bar none told us not to buy. We liked them, though; they were our equivalent to everybody's AC 30s. They sounded like a bag of nails normally but take them into Olympic and they sounded great. I was reading the book I Robot by Azimov at the time and they reminded me of that, little robots that were such a distinctive part of our sound.

We just miked every thing up live, put the drums on a platform and ran every thing out of the control room. It was all done really quickly but it sounded great. We had enough material to choose from, including some of my own songs. We knew everything backwards so it took no time at all. We recorded the first song I wrote for the Buzzcocks, 'Fast Cars', which I was proud of. It was one of the songs I wrote using my old Spanish acoustic guitar, which would go out of tune pretty quickly. Because of that, I started to make up riffs using only one or two of the strings. It was a technique I carried on with right through the Buzzcocks and it affected quite a lot of our songs. Shelley could bounce a similar riff off of it and we'd build on that so I was very pissed off that it somehow got credited to Shelley and Devoto on the sleeve. They did put together one verse but I had ninety per cent of that song down, including the music and the chorus. Apparently, the wrong information got sent to United Artists and it didn't get changed for years. I was unbelievably fucked off because it was a personal song because of that car crash a few years back. They couldn't change the credits until the initial run had sold out and they'd pressed up fucking thousands. I was forever having to justify that song, saying, "Hold on, they don't write every fucking song." Devoto had been out of the band for over a year and he's going to get my publishing. It was frustrating because kids would come up to me and say: "That song was one of the first things I learned to play." I lost out there. It got sorted out in the end and I get the publishing off of the later pressings but you know it's one of those classic mistakes that start off bad feelings in a band, especially once the money starts rolling in.

So that was that. I also had 'Autonomy' which The Offspring have since covered, being new punks and all that.

I'd been listening to the Krautrock band Can at the time and I thought it was funny that they were Germans singing in English. I decided I'd be an Englishman being German, singing in English. I know it doesn't make sense, but it did at the time. I had the music sorted out using that repetitive cascading chord sequence, and I tried to sing in a monosyllabic voice over the top. I don't know if it sounds German but it was certainly different to the more linear punk songs doing the rounds at the time. 'I Need' was bashed out one lunchtime over a few pints down the pub. I had the basic tune and Shelley ran off a list of things he said he needed: I need this and I need that, I need love, I need sex. So fucking simple.

Shelley came in one day and said he had an idea for a song called 'Fiction Romance'. He played me that little chugging intro in E – duh, duh, duh, duh, duh. I'd been listening to Led Zeppelin's Houses Of The Holy album, trying to figure out that track 'Over The Hills And Far Away'. I'd managed to nail it down eventually and there's a bit in that that I thought would fit perfectly. In response to Shelley's riff, I played an open D, which went "Dang dang." So that song's got a bit of Zeppelin in it, especially the little riff towards the end.

'Moving Away From The Pulse Beat' was written in rehearsals at Lifeline with all the drug addicts wandering in and out, off their heads. It was a really experimental number full of weird timings. It came about by accident because the place wasn't really suited to rehearsing because we couldn't hear each other very well. John started off playing a Bo Diddley type drumbeat and Shelley played quite a lot of busy chords over it. Because I couldn't hear the chords clearly, I started playing some Indian-style riffs, which I'd learned on the acoustic. It was very abstract. We had a John Peel session to record that night and we introduced that as a new song. You can still hear me working it out as it went out live on the air. The title was as abstract as the music because it can mean so many things: your pulse moves, your heart moves.

The album title came from some piece in a magazine that actually read "Another housewife stews in her own juices." Somehow it morphed into

Another Music In A Different Kitchen.

We did a photo session at a place called Kitchen Queen, which was a big fitted-kitchen manufacturers in Manchester. We were sat around in these mocked-up kitchens with signs saying "Today's Luxury At Yesterday's Prices" and "Available In Stainless Steel". It was meant to fit into our programme of demystifying the music industry. Stark reality: kettles, toasters and irons. Even our tours had distinctly unglamorous titles. No "Anarchy In The UK" or "White Riot" for us: we had "Tour One" and "Tour Two."

I for one was glad we never went with those kitchen pictures on the album cover. I wanted a picture of us in Olympic with those famous fucking sound screens. Thankfully, that's exactly what we went with in the end: you can make out the screens behind us. We incorporated a bit of the kitchen theme by having a silver finish put on the actual sleeve so it looked like a modern appliance. It didn't reach number one but it charted high at number fifteen, so everyone was happy. For the time being anyway.

It was such a relief to see that album out – and for it to be so well received. We had no idea when we were making it that it would turn out to be regarded as one of the landmark albums of that era. It's definitely up there with all the classic first albums made by the classic punk bands. The Jam's In The City, the Pistols' Never Mind The Bollocks and the Clash's The Clash: they all define the times. I felt we all had something good to offer, something that was individual. It's clear now, when listening to all those four albums, how each band was totally different. We may have all been lumped in together as punks but we were really just great little rock'n'roll bands, the latest in a long tradition. Ours merely had a handy tag for it to be hung on.

Once the album was out, people started to refer to our music as "having the Buzzcocks guitar sound." They still do, in fact. You often read about Brian Jones and Keith Richards and how they practiced forever, perfecting their interaction. You weren't supposed to know who was playing what. Shelley and me, we never did that. It came about like most things did in the Buzzcocks, intuitively. It's instinctive and with it comes this interaction, which is crazy. We both play rhythm and we both play lead and it somehow works out. We can do it without thinking. That album really laid that out because you really can't tell who's doing what and it doesn't matter. It was the bit of magic I was convinced was out there, and it happened by default.

We got some strange offers to promote the album, most of which we turned down. We would always do the in-store promotions and turn up for the record shops like Virgin and HMV. We did quite a few benefits too, like the one for the Electric Circus, which was supposed to raise money for a hospital scanner. I remember the fucking cheque bounced. Another one was for the Manchester Polytechnic's Gay society. One publicity stunt we did get involved in was with the Daily Mirror's Pop Club. They came up with the idea of setting off balloon races all over the country. While we were on tour, we were supposed to pop into all the major cities' Virgin shops and let off hundreds of balloons with little tags attached to them. Whoever found the tag was supposed to send it in to the Mirror to get a free album. Each album would come in a carrier bag with a serial number and a stamp that said "product". More demystifying.

We did one of the balloon things at the Virgin megastore in Liverpool. It reminded me of John Lennon: he did a similar stunt letting balloons go for peace. What made me laugh was, when we got there, somebody stuck about a hundred balloons in my hands and said walk though the shopping centre and let them go up on the roof. So I set off and got about fifty yards when suddenly I felt some bloke's hand in my fucking pocket. I had a load of notes in my jacket pocket and some cunt was helping hisself! I had to let go of the balloons and give him a slap to get it back. Unfortunately, all the fucking balloons had floated up to the ceiling so that was the end of that. Classic scouser.

Having enough money for someone to steal was an indication of how much my life had changed in a short space of time. We'd completed three nationwide tours in less than five months and now we had a few quid. It didn't take us long to start going a little crazy – suddenly there was money for cocaine and champagne. It started in Blackpool, drinking bottle after bottle of champagne. We all had our own coke and, from then on, it was champagne with every gig. Our rider could have been Queen's. One night some kids came backstage and started having a go at me, saying, "How can you call yourself a punk band when you sit backstage drinking champagne?" They were saying we were fakes. I said "Well, I do fuck all else. I don't play golf; I don't go to the cinema, or the fucking theatre, because I don't have time for anything else. I do this all the time. We tour all year." I basically tried to tell them that I didn't have any extravagance while swigging champagne out of a bottle and snorting a big fat line of coke. I thought this is fine because this is all I do, and it's fantastic. I'd got the taste for the rock star life, meeting up with Mick Jones at around that time and doing drugs and stuff. It was exciting. We were twenty-one. Overnight we'd gone from being broke to living the life. We had gone from venting our spleen and anger at the world to 24-hour party time. The live-for-the-moment attitude kicked in because we never knew how long it would last. Drugs go hand-in-hand with that sort of outlook.

We had no idea if we were making punk music history or if we just making something for the here and now. Everything had changed. Suddenly there were girls shouting at me and I was getting recognised in the street. It hadn't started to get on my nerves yet.

Having said that, I made sure I did a little reality check every once in a while. I mean, people were coming up to me in the street and patting me on the back. Everywhere I went in Manchester people would shout out things like "Buzzcocks, great stuff" and yet, a year-and-a-half earlier, I was living in Hartley's asylum. I remembered trying to get a band together, the acid I was taking and how impossible it all became. I'd eventually had to move back to my folks' home because I was so broke and I'd lie on the couch all day reading. My mum and dad would come home and berate me for reading Thomas Hardy and DH Lawrence.

From that viewpoint, it was a lot to take in. My parents were coming home and finding girls sitting on the doorstep. Kids would be outside day-and-night calling for me to come out of the house. It was nice knowing people related to me but it became a problem, especially if you'd been out all night. I used to give the girls old pairs of socks and underpants because they wanted anything you'd give them. They would knock on the door and ask my mum for things: "Have you got anything we can keep?"

They would walk off delighted with an old smelly sock. The neighbours would be standing at their front doors, going, "Ooh, look at him now! Bleedin' pop star, now." It got quite embarrassing but of course I could see the potential in it.

I think being working class, successful and young is a difficult combination to handle. Potentially lethal, even. In order to keep my feet on the ground, I would try and remember that car crash at seventeen and how Alan Hughes died at twenty-one. How we were going to form a group together and how he never made it. I'd think back to that moment watching his coffin go down the shaft and the moment I thought I was going to die. I thought I could live my life for both of us and the only way to tell the story was through music.

I suppose what I'm trying to say is you get out of fame what you put in. Fame alone is no good. Well, it is for the fifteen minutes. To make the music we were making, you had to think about real everyday things. That means the car crashes and the bloke who spends his two weeks' holiday mending it and his wife who's on at him for the bills.

Still, it was hard not to get carried away.

Manchester was a good place to live back then if you wanted to stay reasonably grounded. Which was probably why I suggested we all move to London.

I always maintained we should go, but Shelley wanted to stay in Manchester. His Coronation Street boots where stuck firmly in the cobbles. I felt freer in London: Manchester was a great place but there was only so much you could do. Even later on, when Morrissey started to get noticed, he would get chased down the street in his high heels. He was into the New York Dolls: he would dress up like them and literally have to run for his life. You didn't want that. Full respect to him but, when you lived in a close-knit community, you fucking well stick out in high heels. You step out of your terraced two-up, two-down looking like a punk and people noticed you. I moved in to one of the modern housing estates and it was a fucking nightmare. Bricks though windows and families arguing with one another. It was hard to see the beauty in the world with all that constantly on your back.

I loved Manchester – that's where I come from – but there was something exciting about seeing Big Ben. Watching the Thames and walking down the South Bank, I never get bored of it.

When I was younger I had that Kinks album with the picture of them sitting in a coloured Thunderbird on the front. They were sitting in Carnaby Street and Dave Davies was wearing a big coloured hat: I used to think how glamorous it all looked.

London oozed Rock'n'Roll, chicks and freedom.

Anyway, I was outvoted on that one because everyone else wanted to stay put. We had our office in Manchester and, to be fair, the more successful we became the less it mattered where we lived. We became rootless. Shelley's reluctance to move down to the more happening London surprised me. He could be full of surprises. Something that wasn't so surprising was the little matter of his sexuality. I'm not saying he was openly gay because he'd certainly had his fair share of birds on the road. How can I put it tactfully? I suppose you could say he liked to swing both ways. Fair play to him, it added an interesting dynamic to the group and to his songwriting. We went together to watch the David Hockney film The Bigger Splash and I noticed the place was full of guys and hardly any women. He was trying to explain to me how he liked to get the best out of both worlds. I thought: "Fair enough. It's not my department but I'm cool with it." He was seeing girls at the time, but he was telling me how he was getting more interested in guys. He was fifty/fifty. He used to say to me: "How do you know unless you've tried it?" That's part of his make-up. It was ground-breaking in some ways. More and more things were opening up to us. For him to tell me that seemed like a natural extension of it. That generation was challenging and questioning so much. The Clash had the politics and Shelley liked to tip that field as well so his gender-bending seemed perfectly in keeping. He was questioning his own sexuality: each to his own. He can do what he wants with it. As for me, I wanted to join the Clash.

We toured pretty much non-stop throughout the early part of 1978. We completed tour number three in the spring. Johnny Lydon and his misses threw a party for us at their house in Chelsea.

We did a lot of TV that year, including a programme called Revolver, the show the late great Peter Cook presented up in Birmingham. It was a live show that had featured all the big new wave bands. We did it with Elvis Costello, Nick Lowe and Generation X. It was the first time I'd met them. I dug Billy Idol out as Heinz.

I liked the pop art thing they had going but I always felt theirs was a case of style over substance. They really looked the part but I thought their music was very lightweight. I wasn't surprised when Billy eventually did the off to go solo. He should have covered 'Just Like Eddie', though.

Nick Lowe was doing 'I Love The Sound Of Breaking Glass' which was a straight nick of David Bowie's ' Sound And Vision' but no one noticed.

Peter Cook was fantastic. Derek and Clive was the big cult thing at the time and he seemed to be living out that persona. He was drinking a lot. He had the naked model and he took the piss out of everyone. He came into our dressing room and gave us stick about having a bit of make-up on, especially Shelley: "Oooo, I bet he likes the make-up!"

He could cut anyone down to size.

He was waiting to be seated in a fancy restaurant once and some big shot pushed in, demanding a table. He started giving the waitress a hard time, shouting at her and saying: "Do you know who I am? Have you any idea who I am?" Kept it up for ages, almost reducing the girl to tears. Cook walked up to the guy, put his arm around him and shouted to the entire restaurant. "Excuse me, excuse me! We have a terrible problem here. This poor fellow has absolutely no idea who he is: can anybody help him?"

We also did our first Top Of The Pops around the same time, miming to 'I Don't Mind'. We ended up doing it about eight or nine times in all. Every time we did, I must admit that, unlike the Clash, I personally felt justified in doing so. We met up with just about everyone on that programme including the Jam who probably did it more times than anyone. I forget what single we were doing when the Jam were on but Weller was as angst-ridden as ever, smoking a million fags, biting his nails and spitting on the roof. We had a drink with them in the bar before the show and talked about the Clash refusing to do the show. I said I felt it was the responsibility of bands like ours to do as much TV as possible. It was important we got the music across to as many Dooleys and David Soul fans as we could. To give you an idea of how dire the music scene still was outside of the new wave, consider that 'Matchstalk Men And Matchstalk Cats And Dogs' had been number one. Showaddywaddy still walked amongst us. So did shit like Yellow Dog and Brotherhood of Man. Oh, and – would you believe it? – Julie fucking Covington. She'd come back to haunt us with 'Only Women Bleed'.

Top Of The Pops was a surreal experience in those days. There was always a lot of leopard and tigerskin about. Once I found myself standing next to that little black cat from Boney M, watching the decidedly creepy Dean Friedman. Althea and Donna was number one and the Muppets had their own dressing room. Jimmy Saville seemed like he was on it every week. He had started off as a DJ in the clubs up north. I told him I remembered seeing his name as a kid playing at the Whiskey in Salford. He was wearing Chinese robes covered in jewellery and had his hands clasped in front of him, as if in prayer.

He introduced us as "All the way from Salford."

I'll never forget we were on the opposite stage to the Jam, spaced out and drunk on Pernod and Lemonade. We checked each other out, and mimed our singles. The environment was sterile and the artificial audience just stared blankly at us wearing their Abba scarves. Maybe the Clash had a point.

The things we did for the kids.

Once I'd got used to the idea of staying firmly in Manchester, I eventually got round to buying a house. I was going steady with a girl called Judith Wrightson. We did one day of house-hunting together before I totally lost interest. To avoid another day of estate agent bullshit, I impatiently settled on the last house we saw: 2 Gramby Street. I bought a teasmaid and a globe then went straight back out on tour, this time more imaginatively titled "Entertaining Friends".

It was the heyday of the National Front and Anti-Nazi League. We saw some of their confrontations firsthand. Some guy was stabbed in front of the stage at a gig in Bradford after the National Front started a fight right in the middle of the crowd. The police eventually raided the hall and shut the power off which only made matters worse. Amazingly, Shelley found a megaphone and we finished the gig acoustically, with Shelley sitting at the front of the stage and the entire audience singing along to each number.

At a gig in Oxford, about fifty skinheads fought a pitched battle with bouncers onstage before the police once again intervened.

There was another riot at the Top Rank in Brighton. This time we had most of our gear thrown off the stage. John's kit got smashed and Shelley's amp was nicked, plus we got billed for the damage. It was the last night of the tour. We'd had beer glasses thrown at the stage, so we finished the set and decided to fuck the encore. Bad mistake! The whole place erupted. A tidal wave of bottles and glasses pelted the stage. John Kurd was promoting the tour. He had a reputation as a hard nut. He was on the stage with his crew, punching the shit out of everyone. There was a big metal shell at the back of the stage. The noise of bottles and glass smashing against that and the drum kit was deafening.

We had to barricade ourselves in the dressing room with tables and chairs. It was like Zulu. Oh, how about this for fucking gratitude? We'd given the entire tour support to Subway Sect. How did they thank us? They nicked John's cymbals. Un-fucking-believable. John had to go to John Henry's equipment warehouse the next day to get a brand new set. Cost a fucking arm and a leg. John Henry's didn't stock the type he used (Zildjian's) but, it just so happened, they had a secondhand set that morning. Subway Sect had been in and flogged them. John had to buy his own fucking cymbals back!

It wasn't all mayhem and violence, though. We did quite a few Anti-Nazi League festivals and they normally passed of without incident. In fact, we headlined one of them that year but we let the band Steel Pulse go on last. I played some Reggae guitar on the encore 'Ku Klux Klan'. I'm no

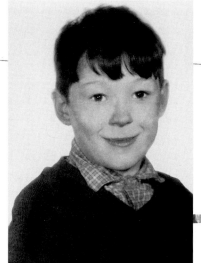

Clockwise from top:
Young Diggle;
Kitchen wear at
knockdown prices;
2 promo shots for
UA in 1978.

Buzzin' all over the world!

Clockwise from top left:
"Hey, Jones!" "Yeh, wot?";
Haven't aged a bit;
T.V. Terrific.

Clockwise from top:
Bored meeting;
A return to the
Hammersmith Odeon;
Harmony in my head.

Above: The essential piece of
touring equipment;
Right: About to hit the road...again.;
Below: Decorated for fighting the
Punk Rock war;
Bottom: Back to my Mod roots.

op: Proudly wearing our
nfluences close to our chests;
above left and right: The Buzzers,
ow with Barber and Baker
candlestick maker not pictured);
ight: Steve and Steve - that's
an Zandt and Diggle.

From top: Shelley and me in 2003;
The Busking Years; The Steve Diggle
Band with Chris Remington on bass;
2003 and ready for anything...well,
almost anything.

Reggae expert but I was in the right frame of mind: I was completely stoned and pissed. The fact I played at all was a fucking miracle – two minutes beforehand, I was convinced I was going to die.

We had been in our hospitality tent for most of Steel Pulse's set, making the most of the rider. After an hour or so, word came down that Steel Pulse wanted me to come on and play a last number. I was pretty pissed-up at this point, plus I'd smoked my way through the best part of a big bag of grass. Still, you can't be rude, so I grabbed my guitar and tottered off. Up the runway at the back of the stage. I was met by one of the Steel Pulse sound guys. He told me to wait behind the amps and listen for my introduction.

I was wearing a pair of Beatle boots at the time, the sole on one of which was coming loose. This greatly aided my unsteadiness. As I bent down to pick up my guitar, I fell back against the backdrop. I realised there wasn't any support behind it as I began hurtling toward the ground. Luckily, scaffolding poles broke my fall every two seconds on the way down and, as the stage was a good eighty feet high, there was a fucking lot of them. I hit my head, my knees, my elbows – I think I hit every bone in my body until I somehow managed to halt myself by grabbing one of the poles about fifteen feet from the bottom. I hung there, stunned and disorientated, swinging by one hand like a fucking gibbon, pissed, stoned and concussed. That's when I heard the announcement over the PA: "Please welcome on to the stage: Mr Steve Diggle!"

I dropped the last few feet to the ground, found my guitar stuck in the mud and staggered back up the runway.

Steel Pulse must have thought I was milking my entrance for all it was worth. I have no idea what I sounded like but I do remember their guitar player shouting, "It's in B flat."

I'd left Judith decorating the house during my absence. By all accounts, she was doing a grand job. But she was fighting a losing battle. While I was away, my brother had rung and asked if he could stay at the house for a fortnight. I said yes, of course. I thought he'd be company for Judith. Being an artist, he could help out.

He was actually making a reasonable living from his art and establishing quite a name for himself as an abstract painter.

So he moved in for two weeks. He stayed for two years. Unfortunately, so did a mate of his, David Heacock the sculptor.

They commandeered a bedroom each and set up their own little studios. Judith didn't mind the painting paraphernalia scattered everywhere, the eight-foot canvases and hundreds of paint buckets. Giant slabs of concrete, tree trunks and a chain saw-wielding nut case, however, she drew the line at. From a creative point of view, the house was a hotbed of talent and experimentation. I did my music in one room, my brother painted in his and Heacock, well… he did his thing everywhere: bathroom, kitchen and garden. He used to wear big round goggles and an old 1950s gasman's uniform, complete with hat. It was navy blue with red piping and sometimes he would replace his goggles with a World War Two gas mask. We would have some marathon drinking sessions that could only begin once Heacock had found a hidden pepper pot. It was a sort of abstinence rule: if he didn't find it in the time allowed, we wouldn't go out and get pissed. He would put his gas mask on, go into the kitchen and search. He never failed to find it. Judith, understandably, gave up the DIY and her colour charts and moved out.

Shelley never liked coming round too often either, as I recall.

I carried on seeing Judith as much as I could but the relationship would have to endure longer and longer periods apart. America was calling.

Before we set off on our first American tour or, indeed, our first European one, we went back to Olympic Studios and started recording our second album Love Bites and a batch of new A and B-sides. We put out the single 'Love You More', at the time the shortest-ever A-side released in the UK. It lasted all of one minute and forty-five seconds. We were also the subjects of our very own TV documentary called 'B'dum B'dum'. We released our biggest hit single, Shelley's 'Ever Fallen In Love (With Someone You Shouldn't Have Fallen In Love With?)', a song inspired by a number in the Frank Sinatra/Marlon Brando film Guys and Dolls. Frank's bird sings a song called 'Sue Me' about him being an unreliable gambler, always ducking out of marrying her. It went to number twelve. We did Top Of The Pops three times, promoting it.

It was a very prolific time for both Shelley and me. We were sparking well off one another and certainly producing some of our best work: 'Operator's Manual', 'Lipstick', 'Just Lust' and 'Noise Annoys' all stem from this period. To give you an idea of how far we'd come: we were asked to perform 'Love You More' on Top Of The Pops before the single was actually out! I wrote our last single of the year, our seventh: 'Promises' had all the classic Buzzcock hallmarks, including Oohs and Ahs in the backing vocals.

It went to number twenty and stayed in the charts for about six weeks.

The album was incredibly well received by the three music weeklies, more so than the first. Melody Maker said we'd "gone a considerable way towards achieving the impossible." The New Musical Express wrote: "The Buzzcocks' prime strength has been their irresistible hook lines. Love Bites is full of ringing guitar lines, beautiful minor chords and choruses you simply can't resist singing." That just left Sounds to say it was "The Buzzcocks purest pop move and, yes, it works." Love Bites went two places higher than Another Music in A Different Kitchen but stalled at unlucky thirteen.

Without catching our breath, we completed our first dates in Europe. It was the first time I'd ever been abroad, the first time I'd ever been in a fucking plane. We went as special guests of Blondie who were breaking big time with their album Parallel Lines. The hit single was 'Picture This': I remember Debbie Harry went everywhere with a little camera hanging around her neck. She even went onstage with it and photographed the crowd – she must have hundreds of pictures of us because she didn't stop using it. I hung out with Clem Burke, Frank Infante and Jimmy Destri: we scored some great coke and bad speed together in Germany. Clem is a fantastic drummer but he really wanted to be his hero Keith Moon. He was the most rock'n'roll Blondie, staying up with me and partying all night. It's funny. I saw him recently and he was clean and sober. I was pissed out of my head. Debbie had a real presence about her. She was a bit Movie-Star-ish: she and Chris Stein never hung with us, probably because John so obviously fancied the arse off her.

We went straight from that to headlining our own dates on what we called the "Beating Hearts" Tour. That kicked off in Dublin and Belfast, where we met the wee Undertones. They were all lovely blokes, bless their little anoraks. They'd asked to meet us and were good enough to admit they'd borrowed a wee tad of our guitar sound on occasion. It wasn't the best of meetings because we were too coked and pissed-up to play the genial hosts. Which was a shame because they were wide-eyed Irish kids doing their best to get away from the Troubles by being in a band. We frightened the life out of them.

The first signs of drink- and drug-fuelled paranoia started to raise their ugly heads shortly after. We were playing the big theatres on that tour – the Apollos and the City Halls - so we were on more money, more booze and more drugs. I had a thing for the publicity girl we had working with us,

Linda Fox. Trouble was so did Shelley. That's when bi-sexuality between band mates can get a bit frustrating.

Not only that: he'd grafted so hard, I didn't feel I could make a move.

We were staying at a hotel in Bristol on one night and there was a huge party going on in the bar. Some rugby team had won some cup and they were passing it round, full of champagne. How could I refuse?

I stayed drinking in the bar for a few hours until, suddenly, I collapsed. I don't know what happened but I hit the floor face first, busting my nose and forehead. The next thing I knew Linda was helping me back to my room. We got in the lift and pressed for my floor: I had my arm round Linda, more out of support than anything else, and we were both laughing. PING! The lift stops at Shelley's floor! There he is, staring at us. That was it. He completely lost it, locked himself in his room and threatened everything from leaving the band to killing himself. Thankfully, Boon managed to talk him out of both courses, but it was a sign that all was not well. I ran into Linda some time after and we got talking: naturally the tour incident was brought up. I finally told her how I'd always wished something had happened between us.

To my surprise, she said she'd wished so too but had been put off because Shelley had told her I hated her.

Just one example of how a very real distance had developed between us. Another thing getting to me was the fact that Pete'd surrounded himself with his own little camp of hangers-on and yes men. And he was experimenting with projects outside of the group.

He'd already put together a sideline band called the Tiller Boys who'd played a few gigs, most notably at The Factory. They were a prototype electronic outfit that played along to backing tapes. Most Buzzcocks fans hated them. To give him credit, I must admit they were a good few years ahead of the game, electronic music-wise. Then again, I felt he should have been concentrating all his efforts on the band. He started talking to the press and saying how desperately unhappy he was, how he wanted to explore the possibilities electronic music offered. He was fond of saying "Punk is dead" in interviews and moaning about feeling creatively trapped by the Buzzcocks. None of which helped band morale. It made John and Paddy feel uneasy. Before I knew it, they were playing the odd gig with other people, too. Shelley's negative quotes started the "Are the Buzzcocks about to break up?" rumours circulating in the press. I was forever having to deny them and try to be positive. Privately, I wasn't surprised John and

Paddy were keeping their options open.

The cracks had started to appear. To be brutally honest, Shelley was starting to disappear up his own arse. He was flexing his ego. Unfortunately for the band, he had plenty of ego masseurs to help him out. He was being told he was the star and therefore he would be okay without us

To be fair to him, we were all exhausted. We hadn't had a break in two years and the amount of intensive touring we'd done had made us all feel we could use some space.

It became a fucking free for all: we had three different members playing and recording with three different groups. John was drumming in a band called The Things, Paddy was in The Teardrops with ex-Fall drummer Karl Burns and Shelley had The Tiller Boys: it was all detracting from the fucking day job. It was ludicrous. The Things were even going to tour with us!

I wanted everyone to contribute exclusively to the group. After all, we were still on the way up. The NME had just printed an article saying so: "After two years, The Buzzcocks have shot to the top." We had the number one single of the year in the Christmas NME readers' poll with 'Ever Fallen In Love'. 'What Do I Get??' was in at number nineteen and the first album was sitting at number twenty-five.

I mean, the Beatles never recorded solo albums while they were together, did they? Well, okay, maybe George did, and there was also the odd Lennon single too. Oh, yes – and McCartney's The Family Way album but you know what I mean.

Anyway, that was the state of play at the end of 1978.

Like punk never happened.

If punk rock in its truest form had started to peter out in 1978, it's safe to say that, by 1979, it had all but vanished.

The Pistols were history. Sid was dead. His ashes were blowing around an airport forecourt. The Clash's second album had been panned as bloated American FM rock. They'd committed punk blasphemy by hiring US producer Sandy Pearlman, the hippy Svengali figure behind hated occult hairies Blue Oyster Cult (the group whose fans had notoriously canned the Jam offstage during the trio's first American outing). However, they still led a motley crew of diehards: the reformed Damned, Generation X and Sham 69. But they resembled a small circle of wagons in a General Custer movie dug in for the big one as a swarm of putrid pop pap surrounded them. The Village People topped the charts, chased by the likes of Racey, Dollar and Sarah Brightman. She was apparently married to a Starship Trooper. The Baron Knights dressed in punk rock clobber and hilariously promised the record buyer 'A Taste Of Aggro'.

Siouxsie and The Banshees were keeping the labour exchange busy with constant line-up changes. The Stranglers had scurrilously offended by releasing a live album.

The Jam were the exception: they were the new bosses. They'd left their (scant) punk pretensions behind long ago and now released their mighty mod opus All Mod Cons, a unashamed nod to all things swinging, kinky and fab.

It was the way ahead.

The Who were back. They'd released their much-hyped big screen adaptation of Quadrophenia, a film and soundtrack that received the sort of media attention normally reserved for big budget blockbusters like Titanic or Lord of The Rings. Within weeks, it seemed the whole nation was in the grip of modmania. Anarchy in the UK, anyone? Nah, mate, we are the mods we are the mods we are we are we are the mods. Groups realised that Punk was as fresh as last year's snow. Those who didn't throw in the towel did their utmost to distance themselves from any aspect of it. There was a shedload of ways to do that. England had caught the nostalgia bug. Beside mod, there was the musical hybrid of Reggae Ska and Blue Beat that spawned the Two Tone phenomenon. That threw up the likes of Madness, The Specials, The Selecter, The Beat and dozens more. No more toying with punk for that little lot.

If you didn't want to go that route, there was still the Rockabilly Revival: Stray Cats, Pole Cats, Hep Cats and Darts. It was a right ole musical hotchpotch. To their credit, the Buzzcocks were remaining impervious.

CHAPTER EIGHT
# BUZZCOCKS
## OVER AMERICA

ODEON HAMMERSMITH Tel. 01-748-4081
Manager: Philip Leivers
STRAIGHT MUSIC presents
BUZZCOCKS

EVENING 7-30 p.m.
Saturday, Nov. 4th, 1978

STALLS
£2·50

BLOCK

22 / R30

Ironic that our next single was entitled 'Everybody's Happy Nowadays': it couldn't have been further from the truth. Not one of our best efforts, it did the trick, chartwise. Once again, Shelley had a basic chord pattern worked out and I played a simple four-note riff over it. Another good example of our two-guitar formula, but a bit clumsy lyrically. Ironically, despite the internal tension, we managed to record our first group composition for the B-side: 'Why Can't I Touch It' was our groove track. I'd been listening to 'Fingerprint File' off of the Stones' album It's Only Rock'n Roll. I suggested to the others we should do a track like it. We all went out to a Greek restaurant and got pissed on ouzo and rolled the tape at about midnight. Everyone played whatever they felt best suited a four-note groove I'd come up with. There's a great middle section with duelling guitars that goes from left to right.

We did another short European tour promoting it and came back for another appearance on Top Of The Pops where Shelley managed to piss me off again.

Sitting in our dressing room before we filmed the show, I told him about an art statement I was thinking about staging with my brother. It boiled down to taking a wheelbarrow full of money into Trafalgar Square and setting light to it. I told him it would be a brutal and symbolic statement that would outrage everyone. Mind you, it was also symbolic of our own accelerating excessiveness. I said for people to flaunt wealth and especially to see money burned is the biggest crime you could do. It was an outrageous idea that Shelley interpreted by performing on the show with a wad of fivers sticking out of his top pocket. He got a shitload of press out of it, declaring, "Money is a fashion accessory." Of course, we never did the wheelbarrow thing but curiously the KLF did it years later. Or did they?

The break-up rumours had reached an all-time high by now so I issued a statement to the music papers, denying them. Although I didn't fully believe it myself, I wrote, "The solo projects currently being undertaken by various members does not mean we're splitting up. It just means we will be twice as busy as usual, plus our manager is losing his hair." It coincided with Shelley producing an album for the band Albertos Y Lost Trios Paranoias and doing a solo acoustic radio session on Manchester's Piccadilly Radio.

Despite all the solo activity, press, radio and TV coverage of the Buzzcocks had continued to grow at an unprecedented rate. Everywhere we went – especially in Europe – there was a film crew. Almost every gig we did seemed to be filmed for some show or other. We did Swedish TV, German TV and Belgian TV (with the Jam). Record sales were going through the roof. Unfortunately, our reputation began to precede us. Our road crew and equipment started to spend longer periods in customs. In Oslo, officers completely ripped our gear apart and the crew were strip-searched. It got to be a big problem because we had to cancel gigs on several occasions and simply fly on to the next one hoping they would be allowed through.

We toured the UK so relentlessly at that point, we stopped naming them, we just turned up and played. Talking of naming things, I remember Shelley finally got around to changing his by deed poll: he was now officially Pete Shelley. Peter Campbell McNeish ceased to be. He also had his house burgled.

Something that didn't happen in homes occupied by lunatics with a chainsaw.

Next up on the Buzzcocks ceaseless schedule was what's known in rock circles as The Difficult Third Album – that and another single, our tenth. 'Harmony In My Head' was my different kind of shot at a Buzzcocks A-side. I wanted to break us away from what I termed our "Mills And Boon" period.

Releasing one love song after another.

I wanted it to be the start of our Ulysses era, to record a single that had a bit of bollocks. My Clash aspirations were still unfulfilled. That aside, I genuinely felt we were getting stuck in a rut and needed to add another string to our bow. I also had a burning desire to show people we could rock out with the best of them. 'Harmony In my Head' wasn't a straightforward story: more a series of images inspired by James Joyce.

It was a very physical and aggressive song and a complete departure from our normal sound. That's what I thought. Sounds said it was "unmistakably Buzzcocks". The NME said, "It is one of the most underrated singles ever." It didn't matter because it charted all the same and gave us another six weeks' run.

The next big change for the band came when it was time to promote it. I was suddenly the front man. Shelley didn't like it one little bit. I hadn't had any positive feedback from him to my songs for quite a while, but this time it was worse. He just wasn't prepared to do for me what I did for him: I always backed him up both in the studio and live but he, for whatever reason, simply couldn't bring himself to repay the compliment. The difference was most noticeable when we came to do Top Of The Pops. It was the show's 800th edition and there was a bit of a party atmosphere. Shelley turned up looking like he'd just rolled out of bed with a day-old beard and – wait for it – a fucking moustache. He stood in the background and did his level best to look as bored as was humanly possible.

So then came the third album, A Different Kind Of Tension or "the Yellow One", as it came to be known. Bands always say if you get past the third album, you'll be okay. You'll treat it as a joke. For us, it was looking more like an omen. John had all but left already for the Things but he was staying loyal to all Buzzcocks duties. Steve had an EP due out and I was even thinking of recording some solo stuff myself. So that's how we entered Eden studios in London.

It couldn't have got off to a more ominous start: the roadies turned up and they hadn't even brought our guitars! Amazing! Never mind, lads. It's only the Difficult Third Album. Look on the spine of an old vinyl copy. It says there: "It's only the third album."

I think we'd made an unconscious decision to forget the singles for a while and concentrate on just making music. We all wanted to experiment but possibly not with each other. Shelley was working within his camp of people. We all were. It was our White Album, each of us working separately, getting our feelings down. The acid was back as well – plus a lot of other things. Obviously, that changed the focus. Shelley was still finding himself and reflecting on his own experiences. I was doing the same.

I was thinking: how do I approach this thing? It became a fucking psychology experiment, with lyrics like 'Hollow Inside'. It was all introspective. I wrote a song called 'Mad Mad Judy' which was about the madness of being on the road. I think the album was more mature and it lot darker than anything we'd done before.

The pop songs had gone – apart from 'Say You Don't Love Me', which was crap. The title A Different Kind Of Tension derived from a record review of the last album that was headlined "Another Kind Of Tension". I assume it was a good one.

Despite the psychosis and introversion, the album entered the chart at number twenty-six. Funnily enough, hot on the heels of a re-released version of 'Spiral Scratch' which had clocked in at number thirty-one. The reviews were actually better for Tension than they had been for its predecessors. The NME said "it has a consistency that wasn't achieved by either Another Music or Love Bites." Sounds even said it was our best effort so far. Melody Maker, on the other hand, thought it was shit.

I couldn't have cared less. None of it mattered to me either way: we were on our way to America. Fucking hell! A dream come true. I used to think I'd never travel outside of Manchester, let alone the other side of the Atlantic. I'd carried around a vision of New York in my head since I was a kid. It was Batman's Gotham city: dark shady buildings and steam rising from the sewers.

I wasn't prepared for the flight at all, a bastard eight hours that seemed like a lifetime. Still, the little bottles of champagne eased the cabin fever and eventually we touched down at JFK.

I was re-tracing those Beatles' steps. Fuck me, I even felt like giving a little wave.

We were also doing it Buzzcocks' style, staying at the Gramercy Park Hotel on Lexington. I was told the Witch from the Wizard of Oz lived around the corner. It wasn't vital information but I thought I'd keep my eyes open. Apparently, she was really old and still rode her bike. She hadn't worked since. I suppose, once you're the Witch from the Wizard of Oz, what are you going to do? I checked in and dropped my bags in the room. No sooner had they hit the floor than I heard two loud cracks, a bit like a firecracker.

I thought: that couldn't be gunshots? Surely not? I've only been here five minutes.

I switched on the TV, checked there was a mini bar and made sure the bathroom had plenty of towels and lots of those little bottles of free things. Check, check, check, and check. Okay, where's the bar?

Before I met up with the others, I had a quick flick through the TV channels. What a fucking eye-opener that was! This was the Seventies. We didn't even have Channel Four yet! British TV ended at midnight: the announcer wished you goodnight and they played the National Anthem. That was it. We were conditioned to go to fucking bed. It was still the dark ages. America had Mickey Mouse going 24 hours a fucking day. It was amazing.

I marvelled at the fifty-odd stations (remote control: another new thing) for ten minutes and went to find the others. I found Shelley in the bar. He was drinking a jug of Budweiser, which we'd never heard of. We were like kids in a sweet shop. There was dozens of new brands: Rolling Rock, Coors and Miller Lite – which, I might add, we viewed with total suspicion.

We stuck with the Bud – stuck with it and stuck with it. After about an hour, I said to Shelley, "How do you feel? Do you feel drunk?" He said, "No, I just feel gassed out." Me too, I thought. I'm not drunk. I'm not happy. I'm just ill. With British beer, you know exactly where you are at each stage of the game, one two three four pints later you still know you're drinking.

You can gauge it. With American beer, no! It only gasses you out. To add insult to injury, it gives you the worst fucking hangover ever because it's made of so many chemicals. I don't think there's a single natural thing in them. It's the beer equivalent of drugs. Anyway, while we were discussing the finer points of the great British pint, two birds that had been sitting in the bar came over to us. They asked if they could join us and sat down. I thought: Blimey, American women are a lot more forward! I think they worked for an accountancy firm and they were on their lunch break.

To cut a long story short, they didn't go back to work and we ended up fucking them on the floor of the toilets. We swapped tops and came out wearing their blouses and lipstick and bumped straight into Miles Copeland. So, how do we know Miles? Well, we had signed to a label in the States called The International Record Syndicate, who were in turn distributed by Miles' label A&M. In fact, Miles was the one who'd organized the tour. He had his finger on the pulse. He was cleaning up in the States with the Police. To make matters worse, he'd brought our label boss to meet us. We were all supposed to go and do a radio interview for the station WPIX because they were backing the New York gigs. We had hoped to make a good impression. Oh well.

The DJ at the station began by asking some fucking dire shit like who's punk and who's not? Is Elvis Costello a punk? He asked if the Police were punk, which brought about an awkward silence. All eyes on Miles. "No, look the Clash are punk," I offered.

When I got back to the hotel that evening, complete with a sodding Budweiser hangover, I switched on the TV and caught the news. I couldn't believe what I was seeing: the cracks I'd heard earlier turned out to have been gunshots after all. Some poor sod had been shot dead twenty yards from the hotel. If that wasn't enough, another guy on the same street had just become the latest victim of some nutcase they were calling the New York Slasher. He'd copped it after breaking down with a flat tyre. The news report said he'd got out to change the wheel when all of a sudden this guy walked up and slashed him to ribbons. All the while, his wife was sat screaming in the car. She saw the whole thing. He then ran off, slashing people with a fucking razor or something equally tasty.

It totally blew my mind. I thought fucking hell! It's a bit tough around here. I used to think Manchester was rough. Talk about welcome to New York. I haven't even been outside yet.

However, needs must. My hangover was pounding so I decided I'd go out and find a chemist shop and get something for it.

That was a laugh. My Batman vision of New York had suddenly turned into Kojak. I was looking left and right waiting for the fucking slasher to get me. Every bloke that walked towards me, I'm thinking: is that him? Is that the fucking nutter? Has he got a knife? Or is it the fucking gunman. Bloody hell, Manchester's a doddle compared to this.

Thankfully, gig time soon came and we were informed we had sold out. The entire tour was. America had waited two years. Our first album release in the States was Singles Going Steady, a collection of all the singles, a Greatest Hits package. The Americans didn't really know: they thought it was our first album. It would have been some fucking debut if it had been true.

A bastard to follow up, though.

The gig was mental. Girls were screaming and invading the stage. The Ramones were in the audience and all the radio and record company people had bought us flowers. WPIX had put up this enormous banner with their name on right across the back of the stage because it was being filmed and broadcast live. All well and good but, right at the end, John kicked over his kit and ripped it down. Oops! That tears it! We were supposed to receive all these flowers from the radio people after the encore. Well, they didn't want to do that anymore. Now they wanted to kill us! Some of the radio guys burst into the dressing room. One of our roadies smashed the first one right in the face. Then it was pandemonium. Security was called. Then it started to get really out of hand. We were rushed out the back just as the police were arriving. I remember Joey Ramone calling out, "Hey, guys! Where are you going?" Sorry, Joe, gotta go. We should have stayed and whacked them but it was our first time.

It was a punishing schedule: three weeks, flying every other day, taking just our guitars and hiring equipment at every gig. We went from New York to Washington (where I smashed my 1954 Gibson) up to Toronto, Canada, for a show at the Music Hall (more film crews) and down to Chicago where we did an in-store. For most English kids, their first time in the States is mind-blowing. I was no exception. The feeling of freedom is totally palpable. And as for the girls! They would just come up and tell you exactly what they wanted. "I want you to fuck me in the butt": they were so liberated and matter-of-fact about sex it made my head spin.

It was in your face (literally). I was used to Manchester lasses, not Cynthia fucking Plastercaster and Pamela Des Barres.

I crammed in every schoolboy fantasy I could think of: threesomes, lesbian scenes, the whole bit. There was even one girl, a teacher, who wanted to be taught a lesson with a riding crop, six-of-the-best style. Ye' Haaar! God bless America.

We had a great show in Minneapolis with the Clash in attendance and flew to the West Coast the next day for gigs in San Francisco and Santa Monica.

I thought we were doing the American thing in style – until the Clash turned up in Minneapolis, that is. They'd been banging away at the States for a while and it had changed them. They still looked impossibly cool but in a different way.

I suppose you could say it was in an American way.

I could tell they were really embracing the place big time. They looked rejuvenated. They were soaking the place up and absorbing it: you've only got to look at the before-and-after pictures. They weren't young punks anymore and they certainly weren't bored with the fucking place that's for sure.

That aside, what impressed me was the fact they had the ultimate in rock'n'roll accessories, in my book anyway. They had a fucking tour bus! The proper silver Greyhound job. Okay, I know it's a sight easier to tour the States by plane but, for the sheer romance of being a young English kid in a band rolling down the highway in your very own tour bus, fucking hell! That's it, that's living the rock'n'roll dream, isn't it? I'd been doing it all wrong, flying over everything. That's not the way to tour the States! We'd been late for every fucking flight so far, running like lunatics and throwing up in the toilets. Nah, I want a fucking bus next time.

We were booked to play the Santa Monica Civic, a five-and-a-half-thousand seater. It was the hot ticket in town and completely sold out. A fact made all the sweeter when we heard Elvis Costello and The Attractions were playing The Whisky A-Go-Go on the same night. Back home he'd always bragged on about how much headway he'd made in the States. The

Whisky holds about five and a half hundred.

For me, this was the big deal. We had the proper Grateful Dead roadies with ponytails lining out the coke (free coke, for fuck's sake! We didn't even have to use our own) and long-legged blondes fetching and carrying and a massive fucking stage.

We must have been thirty feet away from the crowd, yet another first. We were used to seeing the whites of their eyes.

It was certainly a night to remember, highlighting just how different American audiences are to British ones. In America, they don't scrutinise you like they do at home: there's no selling out. Even if there was, who do you sell out to?

It doesn't matter. Maybe you have, maybe you haven't. No one cares. As a musician, it's very liberating. So long as you rock and kick arse they'll love you for it. It opened my mind and I realized you don't have to go around being sheepish and feeling like you have to explain yourself forever.

The American gigs took us to a completely new level. We worked harder and we were more physical – which enhanced our playing. We'd come from Manchester, playing those tinny songs, and America turned us into a world band. Fuck me, I bought a cowboy hat to celebrate.

After the States, life was never the same. England seemed even greyer. Hearing the theme to News At Ten depressed me. I felt I'd been to the moon and back. It was hard to explain to the lads down the pub. I realized that the band had two very different sides to it now: a pop side and an experimental side. I felt we needed to move away from the pop. We started out experimental and I wanted to go back to it. After all, we hadn't intended to write pop songs. They were the only songs we had. The fans bought them and made them hits, which is the other way around to what's expected. I knew we were burnt out. We'd done three tours back-to-back and the songwriting was suffering. We needed a break or at least to cut back a bit. We made a decision to keep it to England and then concentrate on the States. Fuck flying around Europe. You couldn't get drugs in half the places, anyway.

America is built for touring: there's no borders to cross, only state lines, and they don't confiscate all your gear. You just get in the bus and go. It's much simpler. Fuck Europe. That was our new battle plan. The record company had other ideas, of course: they just wanted more of the same. So 'Say You Don't Love Me' was released as our next single and we set off again on one of the longest tours yet. The appropriately named "Tension Tour" kicked off in Liverpool with Joy Division brought along as support.

Straightaway, I knew something was wrong: we were just too fucking knackered. The first couple of shows were laboured and well below par. Of course, the press were on it like a fucking rash.

Melody Maker reviewed one gig as "depressing and disappointing." Sounds went so far as saying "Same old rubbish in a different theatre." It was total bollocks! We may have had the odd sluggish performance that contrasted with those of the somewhat fresher Joy Division but we still blew them off every night. But they were the new industry darlings and, consequently, they received glowing reviews. I thought they were fucking gloomy. The press said the attendance was also down, but we were still pulling two-and-a-half thousand a night. Yeah, that's a really poor audience.

I had a good time on that tour every night: our drinks bill looked like a roll of computer counter foil. I remember Ian Curtis was ill a lot on that tour. He was an epileptic and he had quite a few fits. I never knew when he was actually having one because his normal stage performance looked like he was having fits. We did a few extra encores some nights to allow the ambulance to get away from the venues before the crowd turned out. We had known the band for years. I even took Bernard out to a guitar shop in Oxford Road in Manchester and told him what to buy. I'll tell you one thing: they were nothing like their image of gloom-mongers. Far from it. We did the room-smashing bit with them. We were nearly arrested in Glasgow for breaking into the hotel bar after and helping ourselves, nicking all the flags off the roof and throwing a fucking big shoe-cleaning machine out the window. We played a game of Dare most nights. One of our roadies was a Hell's Angel. Bernard bet him a tenner to drink a pint of piss and he did it.

Ian was a troubled soul on that tour, too. He had a moral dilemma going on: he was married but he confided in me one night about some girl he'd met in Paris. It was really getting him down and he was struggling with it. He asked me what I thought he should do. I said, "Don't worry. Every one plays away from home on the road. That's half the reason you join a band: wife at home, mistress on the road." I told him: "Look, you're young. You're in a band and you're playing rock'n'roll – plus the bird's in fucking France!" He was weighing up his values and morals. I didn't honestly think it was getting to him to the extent it did. I'm obviously not cut out to be a Samaritan: two days later he killed himself.

We had just ten days off following the "Tension Tour" and it was straight back to the States. Before we did that, there was a little matter of putting our house in order, moneywise. John and me had decided we all deserved a bit more money. We'd worked hard and it seemed a reasonable request. All the money went into a central pot and everything was paid out of it. I mean everything: we'd turned over a million pounds in the last few months and the sundries bill was bigger than the tax bill. Alarm bells were ringing. I thought we'd better get our hands on some of our own money fast because the general expenses alone were making us look like Apple. To put it bluntly, money was haemorrhaging profusely.

Boon had revived the New Hormones label following the success of the re-released 'Spiral Scratch' and he was signing up young local bands like The Decorators and Ludus. All very commendable but he was using our money to do it and they weren't shifting records.

Our overheads were massive. The New Hormones office was like a homeless people's drop in. Total strangers drifted in off the street. People I'd never seen before with receipts for all sorts of shit. Roadies were buying blocks of dope as big as house bricks and filing receipts for guitar leads. One of them even bought a car. People were constantly using the phones and helping themselves to petty cash. Morrissey was always in there on the fucking phone. At that time, we had eleven people on the books. It was ridiculous. I don't want to sound mean, but one roadie owed us over six grand. I saw a lot of money come in, but not a lot accounted for. The breakdown didn't add up.

As I said we'd turned over a million pounds that year alone and it was all disappearing before my very eyes. Boon had let it all get out of hand. Don't get me wrong: I thought his heart was in the right place, but his finger was certainly not on the financial pulse.

Okay, I know it's a familiar story. Maybe we should have taken a bit more of an active role ourselves but that's what you have a manager for, isn't it? We'd been so fucking busy, we hadn't given it a thought – wait! Tell a lie. We did have a go at investing some money a couple of years earlier:

What happened was a lot of bands like Pink Floyd and Genesis had invested money in things that were outside of music. Apparently, they made millions. I think Status Quo had a load of diggers like JCBs and Genesis had trucks – or maybe the other way round. We decided we'd set up a PA Company. It all started when we got our first advance from United Artists and we bought a mixing desk. About a month later, we bought another one, then we bought some columns, then some bigger ones and so on and so on. In the end, we had enough gear to fill Hammersmith Odeon. Then we had to find somewhere to house the stuff so we got a warehouse as big as B&Q. That meant more people were needed to run the place because we didn't know where anything was. Then there was the flight cases: we went mad on flight cases. Everything had to have one. We spent tens of thousands with a firm called the Pack Horse Flight Case Company, getting customised ones made in all shapes and sizes. They made us one that housed twelve guitars at a time. We had four of those. We even got one for booze and fags.

I blame Paul Weller and the Jam's fucking wardrobe cases for that particular extravagance getting out of hand.

Then came the trucks to move it, the bloody great articulated lorries and forklifts. What was even more ludicrous was we actually stopped using it after a little while.

We got fed up with sending roadies for things like some fucking pedal I wanted to try for five minutes or a particular amp and then having to wait for hours for them to come back. It took so long to set up a rehearsal, we went back to playing through our little H&H amps. We would set up in this huge aircraft hanger surrounded by a million pounds' worth of gear, using the same equipment we'd used when we started out with Devoto.

In the end, the fucking thing only went out on the road once – when we hired it to the Undertones. It was the only time it made us a penny.

I know it's a cliché to say it was like Spinal Tap but it was pretty fucking close. It was out of our control. At the end of one tour, a driver with a full artic load stayed on at the hotel for over a week. Nobody had told him to go home. Obviously, we should have done something about our affairs much sooner but, no, we waited until everything was in utter chaos before we decided to act and apportion the blame.

And blame we did! It was all Boon's fault! It wasn't really, not entirely, but who else were we going to blame? It was a little unfair and we didn't exactly go about it the right way, either: John and me went up to the office and threw his desk across the room while he was sitting at it and wrecked the place. We told him we wanted things sorted out and all the hangers-on got rid of. I told him I was all for community spirit and helping people out but he was letting people take total advantage. It was clear to me that, if it didn't stop, we were all going to end up fucked. We would have needed a number one record every month for a year to maintain the level of expenditure.

Management wasn't Boon's forte. It had got too big for him and he couldn't handle it. Fair enough. He hadn't done anything like it before. He'd been an art student. Now he looked like he was on the verge of a nervous breakdown, along with Pete. It was a crazy scene, but it needed to be done. Boon probably thought we were being ungrateful. I'm sure he secretly blamed us as much as we blamed him. I think he saw us living like the emperors of Rome who hadn't noticed the place was burning down. I'll admit there's an element of truth in that: we were having the orgies, and the drink and drugs, the coke binges and now it was crystal meth and the first signs of heroin.

Our little showdown over, we left on our second tour of the US. This was to be a much longer trip than the previous one, taking in some of the cities we'd missed out, particularly down south. Pete flew out on Concorde, separately from Steve, John and myself, a decision that heightened tension from the off. We kicked off in Boston and drove (yes, I'd got my bus) to Kansas City, where we visited the famous club Max's, down to Philadelphia and on to Jersey where we were playing a club in Asbury Park called The Fast Lane. Someone said that this was supposed to be the place where Bruce Springsteen hung out. I was down there like a shot. I didn't see him but John was told by the bartender that he was sitting in the Boss's seat. I remember there was a buzz all night because a rumour went round that he was coming down to see us. After the gig, I heard he had been in but I never got it confirmed. I met him for the first time in 2002 and he said he'd gone out and bought the Going Steady album.

So we never got together with Bruce but we did get to hang out with Captain Beefheart (best hash ever) and went along to give Wreckless Eric a bit of British encouragement at his gig at Hurrah's. Then we went back to New York to play the Palladium Theatre with support band, the Cramps.

They were shit! Unfortunately, they didn't know it. They thought they were the bollocks. I think they were meant to do the rest of the tour but somewhere along the line Ultravox crept in. It was their first line-up, the one with John Foxx. I don't know which was worse. Both were bad choices: one signalled the beginning of synthesizer shite and the other thought they were the fucking Addams family. The Cramps didn't like us at all and strutted around, moaning that they should headline. We were blowing them off every night so I wasn't bothered. In the end, they drove us so mad we let them swap. I fucking cracked up when most of the crowd left after our set. I think that's when Ultravox came on board. I did get taken to some bizarre sex shop in Atlanta by one of them, though – which was handy. My kinky schoolteacher was back and some Cramps-like weirdness seemed wholly appropriate. We did dates in Texas and New Orleans and, in the run up to Christmas, Los Angeles and San Francisco.

We returned to New York the week before Christmas, eager to get home. Unfortunately, when we got to the airport some jobsworth decided

Boon's American Express card needed to be verified by their London branch. Because of the time difference, it wasn't open so we had to haul all of our gear off the plane and check into the airport Hilton.

Pete looked exhausted at the end of that tour. He was obviously in a bad way, physically and mentally. I wasn't surprised when he called a meeting in his room and announced that we should all take at least a year off to recharge our batteries. It was a welcome suggestion, one I felt would benefit us all. The only trouble was we didn't do it. We did cut down the live stuff a bit but we were straight back into the studio as soon as we got home. That was our biggest mistake so far. Because of the constant touring, we only had six songs between us, three of Pete's and three of mine. We decided we'd turn all six into the next three singles and call them Parts One to Three. We would release them all in quick succession and do away with the conventional idea of A and B-sides. That was quite simply an exercise in diplomacy. It avoided any argument about whose song was the A side and whose was the B. To get round it, we'd use random letters on the labels and leave it up to the radio DJs to play the side they liked the best.

Looking back, I realize it was fucking commercial suicide. At the time, we thought it was something radical and challenging.

Let's face it: on the whole, DJs are not going to do anything that requires thinking – that's what the plugger is for. His job is to suck up to them and tell them what the fucking A-side is. Back then, boy, did they have to suck! It was the time of the bung, when DJs were treated like gods by the industry. They held the power and they were treated accordingly. Free tickets, free booze, free meals, free fucking everything. It's not like now where an artist can get to number one by selling twelve thousand singles. Bands back then were regularly selling half a million to a million. It was big money, so the DJs were looked after because, if they made your single Record of the Week, you were laughing. You weren't supposed to make their jobs difficult for them – or the plugger's, for that matter. It's like upsetting the postman: your letter goes back in the fucking bag. Still, you couldn't tell us anything. That was our plan when we entered Advision studios.

# CHAPTER NINE
# SOMETHING'S
# GONE WRONG AGAIN

ODEON HAMMERSMITH Tel. 01-748-4081
Manager: Philip Leivers
STRAIGHT MUSIC presents
BUZZCOCKS
EVENING 7-30 p.m.
Saturday, Nov. 4th, 1978
STALLS
£2·50
BLOCK

22 / R30

It was the dawn of a brand new decade, the 1980s. We'd been going roughly five years. Pete's suggestion that we take a year off was right. We were mad not to have done it. We could have sat back and watched what was happening to the music scene around us rather than burying our heads in the sand. The New Romantic era was upon us – as was synthesizer pop. We were sticking to our punk principles. I thought the New Romantic craze was karaoke rock, fancy dress time. As for the synthesizer crowd…

They reminded me of those dreadful cabaret turns you get at holiday camps where you get one guy singing while another sits at a keyboard with all the effects. I didn't see any reason to change our style. The Clash had just released one of the best albums of all time [London Calling] and the Jam couldn't put a foot wrong. True, nearly every one else from the punk days had either broken up or gone skint.

We booked demo time starting at midday with the intent of working through until around eight the following morning. We'd originally wanted to use Martin Rushent as producer but for some reason he wasn't available so we went back to Martin Hannett.

By this stage, we'd reached new heights in excess. We were fucking gone. We may have booked the studio for twelve but most days we weren't actually starting until about two in the morning.

Every day started with the joints, ten to twenty ready-rolled. Once we were totally stoned, we'd need the coke to give ourselves a boost. After the coke, we'd order the acid and finally the heroin. We repeated that on a regular basis until one day Steve simply upped and vanished. He was the only clean one in the band. He never touched anything. Having to endure watching Pete, John and myself get wasted everyday must have been excruciating for the poor sod. In the end, he did his bass parts and fucked off horse racing. Being saner in both body and mind than the rest of us, he'd recently invested in a racehorse called Regent's Boy. That was taking up a lot of his time.

Until it dropped dead, it did. Apparently, the fucking thing broke its neck about two feet from the winning post. He was heartbroken.

The actual recording was insane. We were tripping so much we didn't know what the fuck we were doing. We weren't in control at all. We were doing things that were ridiculous, costly and time-wasting. For example, we miked up everything. We miked up a grand piano and recorded me hitting the strings with a spoon. We miked up flight cases instead of drums, kicked things over and recorded John letting off a fire extinguisher.

I remember doing an interview while we were recording and feeling quite justified in telling the journalist we were every bit as experimental as PIL or the Clash (who were making Sandinista at the time). I spent a hundred quid on a little keyboard called a Crumar from a place called Johnny's Roadhouse, which was a music shop full of nicked gear. It was a complete piece of shit but I thought it was the sound we needed. We had a grand piano for fuck's sake but we covered the tape with that thing. Then came the session players: we brought in Henry Lowther, a trumpet player from Henry Cow, who played this really high-pitched trumpet that pierced your eardrums.

We had a guy from the band Caravan on viola; a cello player called Georgia Born from The Feminist Improvisation Group; sax players… in fact, I think an entire fucking orchestra must have trooped through that studio one at a time. We would be as high as kites, laughing at them trying to figure the songs out.

Then came the Rolfisms: the Aborigine chanting of "Sunderise in the morning." We'd all walk around the studio, Hari Krishna style, chanting Rolf Harris nonsense and recording over the top of it. One day we walked out of the studio chanting and went to the canteen all in a line. We'd been in the studio all night and we were pretty well gone. The Psychedelic Furs were in having breakfast, looking all fit and healthy, and we freaked the fuck out of them. They told me afterward they couldn't get a word out of me because I just made frog noises.

John held his twentieth birthday party in the studio. We got him a big cake and champagne. Jimmy Pursey turned up because Sham 69 were playing at the Manchester Apollo that night. There was coke all over the mixing desk. Jimmy tried to talk me into playing with Sham, but I told him I was far too stoned. Unfortunately, Jimmy's not the sort to take no for an answer. The next thing I know I'm in a cab with my guitar going to the gig. I didn't know any of the chords so I coasted through 'Borstal Breakout' and 'If The Kid's Are United'.

After about a fortnight of that behaviour, we thought that, by some miracle, we had the basis of all six tracks sorted out: 'Why She's a Girl From The Chainstore', 'Strange Thing', 'Are Everything', 'Airways Dream', 'What do You Know?' and 'Running Free'. Well, we thought we had.

'Chainstore' was one of my favourite compositions. It was my sociological question: why was this girl working in a department store? How did she get there? Where did she come from? I based it on something Henry Miller had said in his book Black Spring, which was forget Marilyn Monroe and James Dean and all those stars. Don't think of them as being cultural icons or make them into heroes. His message was the kids on the street are every bit as fascinating, whether it be Junky John, Phil or Mickey or whoever: every one's a character, a hero in some small way, everyday people are just as important. So I made the girl on the checkout the central character.

The song also mentions Berstein's language barrier, which is all about the differences between the language that's spoken in the home and that spoken in the classroom. Some people have difficulties understanding through no fault of their own. They become underachievers. The song ends with the girl in a mindless job just waiting for someone to come along and bite her neck at the disco and marry her. Apart from all that, it rocks along nicely too. It starts with a great chiming guitar part which sounds like church bells. Are they ringing for the life or death of a person, huh?

Deep shit.

When we finally managed to shape up and listen to all six tracks sensibly, it was obvious to every one of us that they needed a lot of sorting out. We were all sitting there going, "What the fuck was that noise? What's that there?" It was a real kitchen-sink job. We had to remix everything so we took the tapes to 10cc's Strawberry Studios near Manchester and set about sorting the mess out. I had every intention of knocking them all into shape. I even got up at six one morning to redo my vocals – no temptations around at that time.

It didn't last long. Before we knew it, we were straight back to our old ways. The porn videos were out, then the joints, the coke and so on and so on. Steve didn't bother showing up at all. John had joined The Things as a full-time member. Eventually, he stopped showing up too. That left Pete, Martin and me, trying to make a silk purse out of a pig's ear. At one point, all we were doing was turning every thing up as loud as possible and then turning it all down again, just pushing the faders up and down. Pete even stopped coming in the end he was so strung out.

Once Pete disappeared, it was just Martin, an engineer and me – until Martin cracked up too. One day he simply got up and walked out the door. He was gone for hours. We eventually found him tripping in one of the cupboards.

We were so deranged by now, we hardly realised that these sessions had dragged on well into the summer. It was the longest period we'd been off the road since we got together.

I was missing playing live. I realised the longer we stayed off the road the more we were growing apart. We weren't really functioning as a unit in the studio anymore. The lengthy lay-off and studio chaos had done little to help band morale. John was now playing regular gigs with The Things and another band called The Renegades, plus Pauline Murray And The Invisible Girls. Pauline used to be in the punk band Penetration and was a big Buzzcocks fan: they covered 'Nostalgia' off of Love Bites on their Moving Targets album. Steve was still playing and recording with the Teardrops and Pete had begun recording a solo album.

That left me down the pub, sitting on my arse.

Around about this time, I got the news that United Artists had been taken over by EMI: they'd become Liberty United. As with all these big takeovers, a clean slate was promised. If that was the case, it was about time I recorded something of my own. Everyone else was.

I decided to do an EP called Fifty Years Of Comparative Wealth, a little parochial EP about British life: "Fifty years of comparative wealth, what does it mean in terms of health?" It was my rebellion record. I was still hitting out at being labelled a love song band. I rounded up John and Steve and the three of us went into the studio. Strange experience: the three of us were recording in one studio while Pete was recording next door. I suppose I should have seen the writing on the wall right there but I still thought we'd be back.

I had four songs, one influenced by a song on the Faust tapes, 'Rainy Days Sunshine Girl', which had a constant bass pedal beat going four beats to the bar. I really liked that so that started me off. The painter Marc Rothko inspired another one, 'Shut Out the Light'. Rothko was the guy who painted those huge canvases all one-colour, maroon. You were meant to look at this big expanse of colour and go into yourself and find yourself. I'd seen his exhibition in Houston, Texas, and thought it was great. Most people thought it was bullshit but I'd been schooled by my brother. It was good for a hangover. Hence: shut out the light.

Another track, 'Here Comes the Fire Brigade', was about the way the fire brigade is used in political situations: "Here comes the fire brigade but there ain't no fire." They're meant to be a public service yet, given the order, they get the fire hoses out in order to quell demonstrations. My take on politics at the time. I sampled a bit of opera, too; thought it sounded dramatic. Either way, it sounded a lot more together than Pete's solo album Sky Yen which came out around that time. It was utter bollocks! Bad Yoko Ono, a load of electronic nonsense that I thought was unlistenable.

Anyway, while I was concentrating on my solo endeavours, the first part of our singles package, Parts One to Three, was released.

For Part One, we'd gone with 'Are Everything' and 'Why She's A Girl From The Chainstore'. It ended up being our worst chart position so far. I think it went in around the number sixty mark.

A gamble that didn't pay off.

Without a nominated A-side, what were people going to ask for? The record shops didn't have a clue, neither did the fans. How we never saw that little problem arising is truly amazing, a testament to how fucked-up we were. We mimed a manic performance of 'Are Everything' on Fun Factory, a Saturday morning kids' show. If you see the clip now, you can see we're not right. We look like madmen. I broke my guitar strap and had to do an over-the-top juggling act with my Les Paul. I look like a nutcase. John gave all his drumsticks to the little kids and about twenty of them were hitting his kit. Pete looks demented. It was a wonder we never traumatised any of those kids. We decided not to do early morning kids' shows after that. We made a video for 'Chainstore' in the Manchester branch of Lewis's.

The poor chart position of Part One should have made us re-think the whole A and B-side thing, but it didn't. I still liked the idea, so we came up with idea of promoting the three singles by playing a short series of gigs around the UK and calling it the Tour By Instalments, Phases One, Two and Three. Each section of the tour would coincide with the relevant single release. Brilliant!

I was happy to be back out again. I thought it was just what we needed to get us focused; it would pull us all together. Amazingly, I still felt things weren't that bad. I certainly didn't think everything was on the verge of collapse.

I could see Pete was struggling with his demons. Then again, so was I. He was very distant on those dates. There was none of his usual between-song banter. John was playing two sets a night because he'd brought The Things along as support. Another good idea that backfired: he was killing himself.

Part Two of our singles plan came out as 'Strange Thing' and 'Airwave's Dream'. It did even worse than Part One, failing to chart at all: our first flop, not that we minded. We took it very much in stride. All the live shows were sold out and we were playing really good.

We finished the first run of eight gigs at the Manchester Apollo – John smashed his kit up and I kicked all the amps over. It was Who-tastic. We threw a huge backstage party afterwards and all our parents came. I felt great that night. We had sold out, we were on our home turf and, as far as I could tell, we were all getting on with one another. I really thought we were back. I had no idea that Steve was looking to form a new group, and was going round saying the Buzzcocks were all but finished.

If he was that fed up, it didn't stop him signing up for another US tour. This time it was more of a promotional visit, not that that was any less stressful: we went straight from Boston airport and did three live sets before we'd even unpacked. We did one broadcast for radio WMBR at twelve o'clock, another for radio WERS at nine thirty and, at midnight, we did a show for WBCN.

We slotted a couple of magazine interviews in between.

It was a ridiculous schedule: radio WMMR, radio WBCN, WVHC-FM. I came down with letter blindness after two weeks. We did do a few proper gigs, notably at the Ritz in New York and the Bradford Hotel Ballroom in Boston where we were filmed once again. I did make time to walk through Central Park to the Dakota building on the off chance John and Yoko were out and about, having coffee or buying a paper. Unfortunately, they weren't but a handful of Beatle nuts standing around in the cold seemed to think they'd be along soon. They reminded me of those old film reels of the Apple Scruffs hanging around Saville Row in all weathers. I spoke to a couple of girls who said they'd heard of the Buzzcocks and thought I spoke in a Liverpudlian accent, then set off back through the park to the hotel, little realising how significant that visit would become.

While we were in the States, we received the cheering news that our publishers were withholding our next advance: apparently we were late delivering the fourth album. That wasn't what I wanted to hear. It had been hard enough to come up with and record the three singles. Part Three was about to be released: so much for the coinciding British tour. Part Three was the remaining 'What Do You Know' and 'Running Free'. It did better than Part Two, but charted really low and disappeared quickly.

We were only back in England a few days when I was woken up in the early hours by my brother with the earth-shattering news of John Lennon's murder. I turned on the radio and listened in total shock. I had been outside his block only days ago, probably right at the spot he was shot. I spent the whole day with my brother and David Heacocks on a massive five-mile pub-crawl. I swear every pub we went in was playing 'Just Like Starting Over'. It was inconceivable to me that we lived in a world where a Beatle could be shot dead.

All our good intentions of starting Phase Two of our Tour By Instalments came to nothing: the remaining dates were cancelled. The official story was 'due to recording commitments'. In actual fact, it was a case of no one being able to face it. It was partly true, though: EMI were breathing down our necks. Cancelling everything in the run-up to Christmas was the right decision. We were being held to ransom by our publishers, so we thought it wise to concentrate on writing some new material.

We also scrapped a return visit to America planned for January 1981. All we played was a solitary Christmas show for the fan club in Bolton, where Paul Cook and Steve Jones turned up and told us about their new band, The Professionals.

Pete and me went out to buy a couple of four-track tape machines in order to record demos. We ended up with two of the first portastudios, a model called Teac 144. They were revolutionary gadgets in those days, allowing us to record separately and, hopefully, get twice as much done. Given that I wanted to make a full-on psychedelic album as apposed to Pete's New Romantic one, this was an advantage.

The sad thing about it was, it needn't have been like that. We could have made a great album if we'd had a side each. It could have worked out great but Pete was not really communicating with me by now. There was no collaboration. We went off in opposite directions.

We had one commitment we couldn't get out of in the New Year,

Germany's "Rockpalast" in Hamburg, filmed for German television. We played a great set with no support. Looking at the footage today, you'd never have guessed that gig would turn out to be our last for over eight years.

But that's exactly what happened.

It wasn't quite the end of us a band. Back home, we were booked into Pluto studios to begin work on the new album. Once again, we asked for Martin Rushent to produce. This time he was free but apparently in America. Word reached us that he was up for the gig and would be back as soon as possible. No problem, I thought. We could go in, start on our little portastudio demos and be ready for him when he got in.

I couldn't have been more wrong.

Pete turned up with hardly anything: he had one complete song 'Homosapien' – dating back to his Jets Of Air days – and a few other scraps. Steve had ordered a brand new bass rig, which hadn't turned up.

Luckily, I'd written about five new songs. We decided to put down backing tracks to those. After two days, Steve's equipment still hadn't arrived. Neither had Rushent.

It was like the Let It Be film: tense. Pete had all but removed himself from proceedings and simply wasn't bothered. We were trying to record a track by Steve called 'No Friend Of Mine' with him on guitar instead of bass. I was trying to keep everyone enthusiastic without a producer. Rushent finally turned up eight days later, by which time I couldn't have given a fuck. He had pissed me off by now. I didn't think we needed him at that point. My attitude was fuck you; you've kept us waiting for eight days, we've been working hard, we'll finish the fucking thing without you.

I certainly didn't need him to turn up and start licking Pete's arse. Straightaway, he was asking, "Where are your songs, Pete? Ooh, we need some of Pete's songs!" It totally pissed me off. The pair of them had done fuck all up till now. If it hadn't been for my stuff, there wouldn't have been anything for him to work on anyway.

Trouble was, Rushent was still drunk on the success he'd had with The

Human League's Dare album – which was a bad fucking sign, I can tell you. It was all drum machines, Fairlight computers and samples of any old shit. Right up Pete's street.

It soon became apparent to Rushent that Pete didn't have any songs. What's more, he wasn't likely to come up with any in the studio. Rushent wasn't happy with that situation. He didn't want to produce a rock album and Pete didn't want to make one. His crafty solution was to whisk Pete off to his own little studio in the country. Once there, they would hopefully come up with something. Rushent told me that, as soon as they got some demos down, they'd come back and we'd continue recording the album.

Yeah, right.

He was so fucking transparent, it wasn't true. I knew he was filling Pete's head with his Human League bollocks. He saw the rest of us as Pete's backing band. In his mind, Pete was the main man so fuck the rest of us. He knew it would be easy to tempt Pete away if he fed his ego long enough. He wasn't very subtle about it. He was basically telling Pete he didn't need the Buzzcocks: he was better off as a solo artist – Sky Yen had obviously passed him by.

It worked. The pair of them fucked off to Rushent's place out in Henley. The rest of us downed tools.

I lolled around the house for a couple of weeks, going down the pub with Judith or my brother. Eventually, I decided to give Pete a call at Rushent's studio. Tellingly, it was Rushent not Pete who came to the phone. He told me everything was going great. Between them, they had some really good demos shaping up. He said he felt that they'd be ready within a fortnight. They'd come back to Manchester and we'd pick up where we left off.

Fair enough.

Two weeks came and went. I rang the studio again. This time the information was a lot more vague. It was all "Oh yes, it's all going well. See you later."

What had happened was this: once they got down there and Rushent realized Pete had hit a dry spot, they resurrected a load of old songs from his Jets Of Air days. It didn't matter that Pete hadn't considered them good enough then because, now, they were getting a completely different treatment. They had all the electronic gadgetry and tricks Rushent had learnt doing the Human League.

Before long, they had an album's worth of stuff. Lo and behold! Pete signed up to Rushent's own record label Genetic Records. I suppose the finished thing is a credible piece of work in the electronic music world, but it did fuck all for me.

Nor for many others. It certainly wasn't the massive success Rushent had gambled on – although I think 'Homosapien' was Number One in Australia.

The first I heard of Pete's decision to leave the band came via his solicitor. John, Steve and myself all got a letter announcing Pete had left the Buzzcocks. I've no idea what the others made of it but I thought it was the most cowardly and underhanded thing he'd ever done. Why hadn't he had the guts to ring us personally? The next thing I know the New Musical Express are on the phone, asking me about the split. They wrote a big news item under the headline "Ever Fallen Out With Someone?"

Fucking right: I never spoke to him again for four years.

# CHAPTER TEN
# FLAG OF CONVENIENCE ABOVE THE HOUSE ON THE HILL

In the aftermath of the split, everything was in utter turmoil. For starters, we had the company finances to sort out, the New Hormones office and record label to close down, the PA and equipment company to sell off and fuck knows what else. EMI issued a statement saying: "All four members of the Buzzcocks are either collectively or individually still signed to the label. That remains the case until any disputes are settled. All work has ground to a halt while their solicitors battle it out."

It was still a potential minefield, one I didn't want to get personally bogged down in. I just wanted rid of the lot as soon as possible. I wasn't about to argue about who kept what amp or what fucking speaker, that's for sure. Besides the VAT and Taxman were sharpening their knifes and circling.

Amid all the bean-counting and legal wrangling, EMI decided to release Fifty Years Of Comparative Wealth.

I decided to move house.

The long-suffering Judith was admirably hanging in. My brother was making plans to move to London and I needed a change of scenery, so I put the house on the market and started to look around for something else. Luckily, I didn't have to look long: Judith's parents, Jack and Carrie, had all ready spotted the perfect place while driving around the countryside. It was a huge rambling Victorian stone-walled house, set on its own land and surrounded by fields near a reservoir. It was fantastic, the mansion on the hill.

Judith fell in love with the place. Putting her art and design degree to good use, she set about doing it up. She did a brilliant job, too, filling the place with old lamps, antique rugs and vivid colour schemes. It really was a dream house and it felt right that we moved in together.

I never did do the country squire rock star bit beloved by so many of our peers, but I did learn to appreciate it. Despite the band breaking up, I was happy. I even tried to get on with Judith's parents who were deeply religious and proper. I'll never forget my first meal at their house: they had invited around twelve family members and friends to dinner in order to meet me. I turned up stoned straight from a tour. I managed not to upset anybody all the way through the main course but fucked it up when the dessert arrived. They brought in a great big tray of stuff, things like gooseberry fool and Pavlovas. Because I was the guest, so to speak, I was given first choice. With all eyes on me, I declared, "I don't eat afters. It's too fucking middle class." The whole table froze. I was never good enough for his daughter after that. He came round eventually but I don't think he was ever entirely happy with his daughter's choice.

I really liked Judith's parents and I was gutted when we got the news that Jack had been diagnosed with cancer. I'll never forget the day he died because he had told me that one of his wishes was to have a piece of classical music played on his deathbed. He wanted to go out hearing it. I thought that was a fucking bizarre thing to request. It would be like hearing your theme song being played like at the end of Parkinson or something: here to play us out is the Royal Philharmonic Orchestra, thank you and goodnight. Fuck that. I'd rather not know when it's coming. I certainly don't want a piece of music announcing its impending arrival.

I was there at the house the day he died. One minute I was shaking his warm hand and saying all those pointless things people say at times like that; the next minute he was gone. I couldn't quite believe it. We left him in the bedroom upstairs as Judith's family milled around doing things. After a while, I crept back up to his room to say my own goodbyes. You never know: just on the off chance he wasn't actually dead. I remember thinking how surreal it was to hold his hand again and for it to now be so cold.

As I was leaving, I noticed his morphine bottle sitting on the side next to his bed. I picked it up and took a swig.

God bless you, Jack.

Grim up north. Again.

There's a famous saying that goes "If you can remember the Sixties, then you weren't really there."

It's a shame the same thing can't be said about the fucking Eighties. Let's face it, wasn't England, politically and musically speaking, paddling up the proverbial Shit Creek? Wasn't it the era that saw a bloodthirsty and power-mad leader impose her policies of mass destruction on the poor of a trusting and unsuspecting nation? Yes, that'll be the one. The caring/sharing Eighties. It was the decade that saw dear old "Margaret Thatcher the destroyer" sell off all the nation's assets (like North Sea oil), kill off the trade unions, close the coal mines and wage war thousands of miles away. The grimness returned to the north as unemployment soared and Norman Tebbit told those who suffered to "Get on their bike" or lump it. Wapping was in flames and the North/South divide widened.

What's changed then? Precious little, scarily – even on the world stage. Iraq was making the headlines by accusing the West of plotting against them by arming Iran. We even had a George Bush lurking in the White House, advising a senile Ronald Reagan.

What was the musical backdrop to such dark and dismal times? On the whole, it was one that undoubtedly deserves the Dark Ages treatment.

Before all you Durannies and Wham fans start to take umbrage at such a harsh and sweeping statement, let's look at the facts: John Lennon and Marvin Gaye were shot dead, Bob Marley died of cancer, the Jam broke up and The Clash disintegrated. On the other hand, we had 'The Birdie Song', A Flock of Seagulls, Kajagoogoo and Spandau Ballet, Frankie Goes to Hollywood. The dance floor chant was 'Agadoo'. There was also the cheeky grinning wholesomeness of New Pop – or white boy funk – where guitars were held far too high and slapping a Japanese bass guitar with your thumb was considered the height of muso chic. Haircut One Hundred and Level 42, take a bow.

Then came the gloom-mongering and shoe-gazing brigade led by Manchester's own New Order, Echo And The Bunnymen and Theatre Of Hate. There was also the new breed of pseudo-intellectual journalists and DJs who denounced genuine working class street movements, like the Mod and psychedelic revivals, yet championed the efforts of the 'theatrical style-over-substance' drivel offered up by the New Romantics. When was the last time you couldn't get that darn Classix Nouveaux or Bauhaus song out of your head? I rest my case.

In summing up the Eighties, one question springs to mind: would the Buzzcocks have prevailed in such an environment? The answer is probably yes. They wouldn't have needed to reinvent themselves to do it, either. That was the fatal mistake made by some of punk's remaining stragglers, the Angelic Upstarts and 999. The Buzzcocks collective and individual side projects showed they were moving with the tide, not against it. Their releases had featured elements of electronics, sampling and programming as far back as Another Music In A Different Kitchen and no one can deny the band's romantic content.

But they didn't give themselves that chance. Instead, the band split in three.

Once the break-up fallout had subsided and the tax and VAT man had picked the Buzzcocks' bones clean, I set about picking myself up and dusting myself down. A new group was the order of the day. My brother had already suggested a name and it stuck: "Flag Of Convenience", a shipping term meaning no allegiance. Flying a flag in the face of the Eighties: that sounded perfect.

It was also another aspect of those times; groups had fucking long pretentious names. There wasn't any Jams or Clashes or a Damned any more; now it was Orchestral Manoeuvres In The Dark, Echo And The Bunnymen, Public Image Limited, and even The Style Council. Flag Of Convenience fitted right in.

I had an idea to keep a common thread running, take a bit of what I'd learnt with the Buzzers and see what the new scene had to offer. Right off the bat, things moved pretty swiftly – not always smoothly but swiftly. John had moved from Old Trafford to a house about a mile away from Judith and me. He was my first port of call.

I told him about the new band idea and asked was he interested. Luckily, he was. A mate of my brother's called Dave Farrow came in on bass, and a guy called Dave Prescott played keyboards: it was the classic Small Faces-style lineup.

Management next: that was covered by Michael Gray, a nice guy who I'd known from the publicity department at United Artists. He had been sacked from UA after the takeover and was now a well-known writer of Bob Dylan books. I remembered he'd always loved the acoustic track off of the Love Bites album, 'Love Is Lies'. He'd said to me once, "If you ever you need a manager for stuff like that, then I'm your man." Now I did, so I took him up on his offer. Sure enough, he got the ball rolling.

On the strength of my recent demos, the first thing he did was get me a deal with Sire records. No, wait: that's not strictly true. Jo McNolte, the guy who ran the American fan club 'Harmony In My Head', had already played my stuff to Sire records A&R guy Michael Rosenblatt. He liked what he heard so Sire signed us and they went with our debut single, 'Life On A Telephone'.

Thankfully, it did pretty well. It didn't chart but it sold enough to warrant a meeting with Seymour Stein, the legendary boss of Sire. He wanted to discuss plans for a follow-up single and an album. A meeting was arranged at the restaurant in Fortnum and Masons and, er... how can I put it? It didn't go too well. Seymour was there with Michael Rosenblatt and all they wanted to talk about was Seymour's new protégée, Madonna and to ask me if I liked Blue Rondo A la Turk. To say we didn't see eye to eye is an understatement. Remember: this was the early Eighties. Everything was based on looks: everyone had a fucking mullet and wore peg trousers and eye-shadow.

The music was secondary. Bands like Visage and Japan: it was all shit. I wanted to release the next single in a classic seven-inch bag with no frills.

Seymour wanted it to have the all-singing and dancing twelve-inch treatment. Twelve-inch singles were the big thing then: everyone had to have them, with additional mixes of the same song on the B-side. I just wanted the label's logo. I told them I wanted to do an album like the Stooges and call it The Accused. Wrong thing to say. They looked at each other and said that was far too ominous. It was all downhill from there. I said, "Look, you've had your pop single, now I want to get a bit darker, heavier." Business-wise, I wasn't playing the game. That wasn't what they wanted to hear. They wanted another Culture Club but I stubbornly stuck to my guns,

The meeting politely fizzled out. I was left sitting at the table with Michael, thinking, "Ah ah, that's the end of that little relationship!" I looked at him and said, "Fuck, it's all over for the likes of me, innit?"

There was another single, 'Changes', and another line-up. John was still with me, but two new guys called Mark Burke and Gary Hamer joined as a second guitar and bass player. They came via the time-honoured tradition of placing an ad in the Manchester Evening News. Mark only stayed for the one record but Gary would turn out to be the band's mainstay over the next couple of years.

'Changes' was the first single in a series of faintly autobiographical record releases. It was about the changes in the music industry and the changes within oneself: the struggle of change. It had a line that went: "In your life things disappear, what you see won't be here next year."

That was particularly true of Sire Records. They'd let us go during the recording of 'Changes', causing the band to break up.

John had had enough. It was obvious to both of us that we were out of sync with what was happening, especially in England. I was trying to shoehorn an R&B band into the wine bar and cocktail era. It was all about style, make-up and drag queens. All those early Eighties bands wanted to be seen as glamorous but most of them looked like bricklayers with a lot of slap on. Some even tried to say it was a reaction to and a backlash against the greyness of the Thatcher years, but it had more in common with Dame Edna and Barbara Cartland. I suppose Spandau Ballet had a few tunes but, on the whole, it was lightweight Saturday-night-at-the-London-Palladium crap.

It was becoming apparent that, unless I wore a fucking dress, I wasn't going to get a deal. We didn't stand much of a chance, certainly not far as another major was concerned.

John was a lot more disillusioned with the music scene than I was. He'd been getting involved for some time with the dragster racing. He started out fixing Volkswagen beetles and going to VW meetings, the ones where hundreds of Volkswagen owners get together in huge field and check each other's camper vans out.

From there, he started going to Santa Pod and hanging out with all the dragster guys. He took me to a couple of meetings. They went on for fucking hours. I couldn't understand it – all these skinny long cars, with fucking great jet engines on the back that only went about a hundred yards. Some of them were fucking enormous. I would be sitting there thinking, "Oy, oy, the next two look a bit tasty." There would be all this fucking smoke and noise and then, "Whoooooooosh!" Another hundred yards. It's the motoring equivalent of a two-minute shag. Still, John loved it. He's doing great with it. He's now a big player on the dragster circuit and runs his own business: John Maher Racing.

And me? I went back to basics, back to the beginning.

What else was I going to do? I put yet another line-up together, this time without John (which was strange after so long), and signed to MCM, the Cartel independent. I had come full circle, forming a little independent band that was paying for itself and signing to a little independent set-up. It wasn't glamorous, but it felt good.

As for getting a stable line-up, that wasn't so good. Gary was still on board but, from here on in, people would come and go so often it felt like the labour exchange. At first, I wanted musicians rather than characters – which was wrong. I could have had some great guys from well-known bands that had broken up, but I went for faceless types.

We'd put ads in the paper and arrange to meet the applicants outside pubs and stuff. Gary and me would drive past first to see if we liked the look of them. Most of the time, we just kept on driving. They all looked like they had come straight from Roxy Music. I don't know why but I had this idea that I still wanted to be one quarter of a four-piece band.

What I should have done was call it "Steve Diggle" right from the very start because I ended up with people with no identity whatsoever and it wasn't working. I mean McCartney called his second band Wings but do you think anyone cared who the fuck was in it? I eventually changed the ad to read: "If they could drink with us all night, then they would get an audition."

We never really did get a settled line-up in Flag Of Convenience despite releasing a string of singles and three albums during the Eighties. The longest-serving member besides Gary was John Maher's replacement, John Crane. John was one of the few real characters to pass through the band's ranks. He came from a very theatrical family background and was a proper English eccentric.

The first thing he played on was the single 'New House', a self-explanatory little number about rebuilding your life and getting your house in order. Which, I'm sorry to say, was something I wasn't doing at all. In fact, I was doing the exact opposite.

Keeping a band with an ever-changing line-up on the road was getting me down, especially as we relied on gig money to survive. Consequently, if we weren't auditioning new players, I was on the road. I was spending more time away from home than ever, still drinking heavily. My substance intake was hitting a new high, or should I say low. It had become a never-ending spiral, one that threw up all manner of headaches at home and on the road. The constant touring meant the gaps between releases got longer and the bands ever-changing personnel meant we never built up a stable identity.

Another setback occurred when Michael Gray upped and left.

He'd got a better offer from Gerry Rafferty. I can't blame him for that. His timing there was perfect: he took over as manager just in time for the release of 'Baker Street'.

I heard he went back to his old label and hit them hard in the wallet after that.

By the time we came to do our first real album Northwest Skyline (there had been a cassette-only release called "The Big Secret"), I'd scaled the band down to a more manageable three-piece: Gary, John and me. John Maher guested on two tracks. We recorded it at a studio in Salford called the Old School, right next door to The Smiths who were laying down their first demos.

Northwest Skyline was my 1960s kitchen-sink drama album. I wanted it to be the musical equivalent of one of those great paperback novels or films: Saturday Night, Sunday Morning or Poor Cow. It was my take on life in the north. We did the sleeve in black-and-white. Instead of Albert Finney leaning on a lamppost, I leaned against an old chimney. There's also a picture of Gary on the inside, running out of a police station. The songs have enough of a thread running through them to make it conceptual. It starts with the line: "As the sunset time on poverty and crime, you lose your mind over the Northwest skyline." I was (am) really proud of that album. An interesting contrast to how I felt about myself at the time.

A few years had passed since the Buzzcocks split and none of our paths had really crossed. I'd stayed in touch with John on and off but not with Steve or Pete. I suppose I was still pissed off. I'd seen Pete just once, one night in the Hacienda. I was amazed at how old and lost he looked. I said to Gary, "Just wait and see: he'll come knocking on my door eventually."

I hadn't kept up with his solo activities. Every now and then someone would give me a snippet of news. Things like the 'Homosapien' single being banned by the BBC because it was considered to have gay overtones. I heard he'd done a solo tour in the States with Steve Garvey called "The Man And Machine Tour." He was still farting around with computer technologies: they did the tour using a backing tape, which sounded like another Martin Rushent collaboration to me. Steve settled in America after that tour and tried to put a band together called Motivation who, by all accounts, had similar line up problems to Flag Of Convenience. The last I heard was he married and working somewhere in New York.

There was a flurry of renewed interest in the Buzzers during the latter part of the Eighties thanks to Fine Young Cannibals' cover of 'Ever Fallen In Love?' It went top ten after it was featured in the film Something Wild, prompting EMI to re-release the Singles Going Steady album. When that charted, they followed it up with all the original albums pressed on blue vinyl. Suddenly everybody was name-dropping the Buzzcocks, citing us as an influence. Bands like the Soup Dragons, Orange Juice and The Smiths were all singing our praises. Pete was even asked on The Old Grey Whistle Test if we were reforming.

I decided to take full advantage of our well-deserved re-evaluation to re-launch Flag Of Convenience under the abbreviated title FOC. Those re-issues had breathed new life into me and the ole bank balance.

I got a new manager in Howard Jones (manager of the Hacienda), a new guitar player in Andy Couzens and, with drummer Chris Goodwin, we hit the road once again. First stop was France and the Locomotive club next door to the famous Moulin Rouge. I hadn't been in France for a while so I wasn't expecting too big a big crowd, maybe a walk-up of two hundred or two-fifty. When we arrived, I was shocked to see a huge crowd milling around outside. It had swollen to around two thousand by gig time. I couldn't believe it. I thought, "They've got the wrong fucking night, this lot." I picked up one of the club's flyers and it all became clear. The scales fell from my eyes! I read "The Buzzcocks/FOC": the crafty French promoter had taken a liberty with the gig's billing.

It was totally misleading and well out of order, not to mention potentially hazardous to my health. I certainly didn't fancy a couple of thousand French punters turning nasty when I walked on the stage with three unknown blokes in place of Shelley, Maher and Garvey. I was really pissed off so I grabbed hold of the promoter and politely pointed out that he had misled every one. It was obvious he had chanced his arm and that the majority of the crowd had paid to see the fucking Buzzcocks. In case he hadn't noticed, they weren't fucking here.

It didn't do a blind bit of good. How could it? The place was already packed and the promoter wasn't about to offer a refund, was he? There was only one thing to do: get fucking drunk at his expense. "Champagne, my man!" By the time we were due on, I was legless. I remember having to empty three ice buckets into a sink and putting my head in it, trying to shock myself sober.

I have no idea how I pulled off that gig because we didn't play one Buzzcocks song – not because I didn't want to but because we simply hadn't rehearsed any. It was such a fucking relief to hit that final note and say good night, I can tell you. Not that that was the end of it. The nightmare was just beginning. We found out backstage that all the European gigs were billed the same way! Apparently, the promoter had checked, and found out that nobody actually owned the name Buzzcocks. Incredibly, it had never been registered. That meant anyone could use it. As he smugly pointed out, he was perfectly within his rights to do so. The same thing had happened to Fleetwood Mac in the early Seventies when a second version of the band toured America without Mick Fleetwood or John McVie, or any other original member.

That's fucking typical, I thought. We never even owned our own name. The tour continued through Germany and Sweden. Sure enough, we were advertised as "The Buzzcocks/FOC" everywhere. I wasn't happy with the situation because I didn't want anyone to think I was trying to live off of past glories or even pass ourselves off as something we weren't. That aside, we were selling out every gig which went someway to curbing any feelings of dishonesty I might have harboured.

What I hadn't bargained for was the fact that, by the time we got back to England, word of the Buzzcocks playing on the Continent had spread like the flu. I had assumed no one at home would have been any the wiser about the double-barrelled cock-up. I'd thought, with Europe out of the way, that would be the end of the matter.

I couldn't have been more wrong.

Rumours that the Buzzcocks were about to reform were rife – and not just at home. Miles Copeland's brother Ian had an agency in America called Frontier Booking International or FBI. He rang from the States to find out if it was true. That's when I knew some sort of shit was about to hit the fan.

I wasn't wrong. The next thing I get is a letter from Pete's manager threatening me with all sorts of reprisals if I continued to use the Buzzcocks' name.

Now, I hadn't intended to use it anyway: but I knew no one was going to believe the French promoter story, so I took a leaf out of his book and went on the defensive. I rang up Pete's manager and basically said, "If you want to stop me, you're going to have to come down here personally. I'll be waiting."

The thing was: Pete was doing fuck all at that point. He certainly wasn't using the name – neither was John or Steve. Therefore, I thought, if they're not using it, I'm as entitled to it as anyone.

What started out as a semi-innocent scam on the promoter's part was now a major bone of contention. I chose to ignore the threats from Pete's camp and we set out on a short English tour playing small club dates up and down the country. There was a big benefit show in Halifax, to help raise money for the rain forest and even a twelve-inch EP released under the Buzzcocks/FOC banner called 'Tomorrow's Sunset', all of which added to the tension.

It didn't chart, but it had a great Jackson Pollock-styled cover not dissimilar to the Stone Roses debut – which did chart.

Thankfully, all talk of legal action fizzled out after those initial threats. It seemed life was settling down and getting back to normal. Gary and me were once again without a rhythm section after I had a falling-out with Andy and Chris and sacked them. Not that it was an immediate problem because our plans to record a follow-up album to Northwest Skyline were on temporary hold anyway. Gary was taking some well-earned paternity leave as his girlfriend was just about to give birth. I fully intended to spend some quality time at home with Judith.

Then came the phone call.

It was Pete's manager Raff. It transpired that Pete had received a call from the persistent Ian Copeland. He was offering a shitload of money for a Buzzcocks reunion tour of the States.

Unbelievably, Pete had already agreed, in principle, if he could convince the whole band to join him. I thought, "Fucking hell, he's still getting people to speak for him. That's a shit start right there." Raff said Pete was up for the tour but he wanted to know if I was. He also wanted me to sound out John and Steve.

As it happened, I didn't have to. Ian had already tracked the pair of them down. Apparently, they were both saying the same thing: "I will if you will." This went on for a few days until all four of us agreed. I don't remember who told who first, or where and when. Somehow an arrangement was made whereby we'd all converge on John Henry's rehearsal-and-hire complex off the Pentonville road in London within a fortnight. I can't tell you why any of the others agreed to do it – apart from the money, of course – nor can I vouch for their level of commitment. All I can say is I, personally, had absolutely no intention of staying around any longer than necessary. I'd be lying if I said I wasn't curious about meeting up again after so many years, but I promised myself that, at the first signs of any egocentricity, I was off.

When the day came, I was excited but very apprehensive. Eight years is a long time. I figured that grudges and misconceptions either fester or fade.

We were told to be at John Henry's for twelve. I arrived on the dot. I pulled into the yard at the same time, amazingly, as Pete and John. It was the first time since we'd met that we'd ever done that. Okay, Steve was late but he had a long way to come. We all got out and nervously hugged and shook hands. I remember thinking, "That weren't too bad." We were shown to the big rehearsal space that John hired out to bands that were preparing for long tours. It had a proper stage set-up with a wall of mirrors in front so you could practise your moves to get an idea of how it all looked. It was strange seeing our old logo taped to the big soundproof doors and all the gear set up exactly the same way we'd arranged it all those years ago. We decided we'd wait for Steve, who'd flown in from New York the previous evening, before plugging in so we sat around talking small talk. Steve eventually arrived looking every bit as fit and healthy he always did – yet somehow he was different.

I couldn't put my finger on it at first so I busied myself tuning up. John adjusted his kit. Then it hit me: Steve was talking in an American accent. Pete had already clocked it and was standing there with a big smile on his face as Steve spouted on about sidewalks and freeways, oblivious to all three of us eyeballing each other and mouthing, "He's from fucking Prestwich, the cunt."

Then the moment of truth came as we counted in our first number and hit the opening notes. I honestly can't remember what song we chose that day. What I do remember was that it sounded incredible. As if we'd never taken a break. Nobody missed a beat and everybody knew their cues. It genuinely shocked all four of us: how easily it all came flooding back! I can't remember what song we did next either but I know we played it as effortlessly as the first, and then… we stopped.

You see, there was a bar in John Henry's. After just two numbers, we adjourned to it and stayed there for the entire session. It was great, just like old times: grievances were forgotten and friendships renewed. We had a full week's rehearsals booked so, as the night drew to a close, we arranged to meet back at the bar the following day at twelve. There was a lot of back-slapping and laughter in the car park and I left a very pissed but happy man.

Unfortunately, that first day set the tone for the rest of the week. On the second day, we did one number before adjourning to the bar. After that we never set foot in the rehearsal space again. We would go straight to the bar each day and that would be it. Steve knew the pattern only too well and would turn up for about an hour and then leave. Pete, John and myself would go for the long haul. In the end, even John said fuck it, we'll see you at the airport. Déjà vu. The Buzzcocks were back.

The night before I left for America, I phoned Gary and told him I'd see him in four weeks' time. When I did, we'd book some studio time and start the new album. Of course, that never happened. Those four weeks turned into another fourteen years.

Before I knew it, I was back in New York throwing my bags into my room and boarding a bus that was taking me to the first Buzzcocks gig in eight years.

# CHAPTER ELEVEN

# THE BUZZ WAGON ROLLS AGAIN

ODEON HAMMERSMITH Tel. 01-748-4081
Manager: Philip Leivers
STRAIGHT MUSIC presents
BUZZCOCKS

EVENING 7-30 p.m.
Saturday, Nov. 4th, 1978

STALLS
£2·50
BLOCK

22 / R30

The tour was billed as the "Telling Friends Tour". It went down brilliantly: nineteen dates in as many days and back home for Christmas. We did a further seven British shows – billed as the "UK Reunion Tour" – ending with a gig at Nottingham's Central TV studio to be broadcast at a later date. We also got the news that John was packing it in once again.

I was sad to hear he was going and a little bit surprised – after all, our profile and finances were at an all-time high. You could've said the Buzzcocks were arguably bigger than the Buzzcocks. We were enjoying playing together and getting on with each other better than ever. Still, he had made up his mind. He had too many commitments to his drag-racing business to risk doing another year of touring. Unbeknown to me, that is exactly what lay ahead.

John had made commitments and I understood that but I'll tell you something, they paled in comparison to the one I was facing up to. Believe it or not in between the constant touring, I had found enough time to become a Dad. Judith had just given birth to a perfect baby boy who we called Jack James. We were both over the moon. It's still my proudest achievement. I thought it would be the beginning of a new phase of my life. Looking back, Jack's birth should have been an almighty wake-up call. But, much as I loved him and Judith, it didn't stop me signing up for another fucking tour.

Nowadays I realise even considering going back on tour wasn't the most thoughtful thing I could have done. To say the fucking least. I convinced myself I was doing it for all the right reasons: we could always use the money, it's only another four weeks...

Luckily, John's departure wasn't the nightmare I envisaged it being because Mike Joyce of the recently disbanded Smiths came to the rescue. He was an absolutely ideal replacement: a fellow Manc who had been a huge fan of the band first time around. He told me the reason he took up the drums in the first place was because he was so inspired by John's playing. Mike joining was good for all concerned. He was a strong powerful drummer and his playing brought a fresh feel to the songs. He was also well-known because of the Smiths. It was almost as if we were carrying on a bloodline between two different generations of Manchester's finest.

Mike's first gigs with us were on the 1990 Australasian and Japanese tours, the beginning of two years' constant roadwork. We toured non-stop, back-to-back UK, America, Europe and the Far East tours, far harder than anything we did during the 1970s and early 1980s.

EMI, never slow to spot a tie-in opportunity, released our entire back catalogue as a box set called Product, which came with the biggest fucking bar code I'd ever seen, courtesy of Malcolm Garrett's minimalist art work. It also came with a 48-page booklet in which Pete spoke openly about our coke and heroin use. I naively thought that surprised a few people because up until that point I thought nobody had any idea.

We also played our first-ever Reading Festival along with fellow 1970s veterans the Fall and Wire.

In between the constant touring, we unwisely snatched a bit of studio time at Drone Studios in Manchester, with the intention of putting down a handful of demo ideas earmarked for a comeback album. I say "unwisely" because we hadn't really had time to write many fully formed songs. I was still clinging to a vague notion of eventually resuming my solo career so I used some of the time to record my own material, using just the producer. I put down a handful of songs like 'Wallpaper World' and 'Wednesday's Flowers' which I didn't think suited the Buzzers and decided to save them for a later day.

The four of us did record some stuff. In fact, we had the basis of a really good album but, if there was one thing we'd learned last time around, it was never try and record on the run. When we listened to the playback, everyone agreed the new material sounded far too rushed and half-baked. Rather than spoil the present run of good luck, we decided to put the whole thing on hold, at least until we had a proper break in our schedule to do the new songs justice.

We did release a live EP of new songs on a hastily set-up label we called "Planet Pacific" but, with no promotion, it slipped out unnoticed.

After another series of UK dates in early 1991, we returned to New York to begin another trek across the States. I think that particular outing was one of the most outrageous, even by our standards. Or was it the next one? Either way, it was one of those early 1990s jaunts that should have been called the "Pure Decadence" Tour.

We were staying in the top hotels and eating in the most expensive restaurants we could find. I treated the whole trip as a personal Rock'n'Roll odyssey, staying in the Toronto hotel room that John and Yoko used for their Bed-In and in John Belushi's bungalow at the Chateau Marmont hotel in California (Number Three, fact fans).

The Chateau is probably the most Rock'n'Roll hotel development in Los Angeles. It's on Sunset Boulevard and you can hire out all these little private cabins on the grounds. Everyone's stayed there, from Elvis to Zeppelin. It's like the Chelsea Hotel in New York or The Columbia in London. They've all got a lot of history: the Chateau had John Lennon's piano in the reception area which I had a little tinkle on – and I did a phone interview to some radio station while receiving a blow job.

There was one scary incident during the tour: at a high-rise hotel, some drugged-out fan hung by his fingertips from my balcony about fifteen floors up.

I was shagging some bird over the balcony rail when all of a sudden she let out this almighty scream. I looked down and there was this fucking nutter grinning up at us between her legs. He had somehow leapt from the balcony below and was now inching his way around ours at feet level. I couldn't do a thing because he had got himself into the perfect position right at the crucial moment; and then he was gone on to the next one.

It was a great pleasure to get to know R.E.M. on that tour. We met when they came to see us at a gig in New York and we hung out at Tramp's afterwards. I went out to some club with Peter Buck the next night, to watch Michael Stipe sing a couple of numbers with a band he knew. Peter's a great bloke and he can really push the boat out. Well, he did then! We were having a great night until he mysteriously disappeared; he was gone so long I just assumed he'd left for home, until he suddenly reappeared looking like shit and told me he'd spent the last three hours with his head down the toilet.

He turned up at the hotel the next day with a little bag of plastic Keith Richards skull rings and gave us all one each.

We returned to England around August, fully intending to take some time off but, like a lot of hard-touring bands, we found it hard to wind down so we played an open-air gig in Manchester's Heaton Park and accepted a further three months' work back in the States. We also booked two weeks in New York's Green Port Studios with producer Bill Laswell and set about reviving the album. The sessions went well enough. We recorded over fifteen tracks but, for one reason or another, they just weren't happening. At the end of the fortnight, we scrapped the project once again. All that stuff is still laying around on a DAT tape somewhere. It's never seen the light of day, which is a shame because, even if most of it wasn't up to scratch, it's still an historical Buzzcocks document. It turned out to be the last thing Mike Joyce did with us.

Mike had made commitments. He wanted to keep busy, and believed us when we said we were taking time off. Rather than sit around waiting for us to get back to work, he signed up with Johnny Lydon's PIL for an album and a tour. That left us with the dilemma of cancelling a European and Japanese tour until a phone call to John Maher saved the day.

John valiantly agreed to cover the endangered dates for us – so long as we understood he was off back to the track directly afterwards. It was great to have the old band back for one last trip. John had a really good time on that tour: he even managed to take in a few race meetings along the way, hanging out with pit crews and mechanics backstage. For a minute, I thought maybe he was back for good, but he stuck to his guns. No sooner had he hit his last drum than he was off.

He knew us well enough to know that, given half a chance, we'd try his loyalty and extend those initial dates by sneaking in a few more – like a tour of Australia, for instance.

Well, it's practically next door to Japan, isn't it?

John wasn't going to fall for it. We reluctantly cancelled the first six dates while we tried frantically to fill the vacated drum stool.

We salvaged the best part of the tour using a drummer called Steve Gibson who was with the band The Icicle Works. I think he went on to Tears for Fears – or was it the other way around? He was quite a good drummer but totally inappropriate for us. He was like a metronome. His playing only underlined how important it was for us to get a permanent replacement.

That was now our biggest priority. Or so we thought.

It turned out our personnel problems were about to double: at the end of the Oz tour, Paddy Garvey informed Pete and me that he too was finally knocking the Buzzers on the head.

I understood his reasons. He was married and lived with his wife in New York. They had two young kids and he was missing them grow up. He had responsibilities and commitments which Pete and me were either ignoring or, worse, not facing up to. To all intents and purposes, we were still living the single rock'n'roll life. I, for one, could see no reason to stop. I was sorry he was going but equally determined to carry on, even if we were down to a two-piece. Steve returned to America. He took a job in the docks before moving with his family to Philadelphia where he still lives, working as a carpenter.

It was back to the rehearsal room for Pete and myself. A week of auditions. Auditioning drummers is the worst: they normally don't care who they play for. They'll play any style you want to get the gig. There are exceptions but, on the whole, it's difficult to gauge if they like your stuff or not. Normally, the only way to find out is to hire them. That's a risk. That's the attitude I started the auditions with. I wasn't wrong. The first bloke who turned up was the drummer with the fucking Glitter Band!

It was agony. Pete and me went though the motions regardless, but it was clear he didn't have a clue. If I'd known a Glitter Band song, I would have played it, just so he could've kept up. Once it was over, we said our goodbyes, lying through our teeth that we'd let him know. As he was leaving, the second applicant arrived. It seemed to me they knew each other. Then I remembered: the Glitter Band had two fucking drummers! We went through dozens of drummers and bass players but none of them were suitable – apart from one Scottish drummer. But a Jock in the Buzzcocks didn't seem right. He never got the call.

It was all looking a bit bleak until Tony Barber walked in and said, " Okay, which one of your songs do you want me to play?"

He knew them all note for note – it was amazing. He even reminded us of a few. As luck would have it, he'd brought along a mate called Phil Barker to back him up on drums. He was good as well so we took two for the price of one.

We did two days' rehearsals at John Henry's and debuted the new line-up at London's Town and Country Club in September before flying to France and headlining the St Quinten festival.

1993 kicked off with another European tour and a spot of solo recording. I released an EP called Heated And Rising. The Buzzers signed a deal with Castle Communications. With a new label behind us, we finally got down to re-recording all the songs we'd scrapped or stockpiled over the last year-and-a-half. The result was our long-awaited fourth album, Trade Test Transmissions.

I anticipated a complete media backlash to greet it. The music press (British, in particular) hates comebacks of any sort. They love to encourage groups to reform and then delight in rubbishing them as old farts who should have known better. Look how they went on about the Clash!

It's common practice for them to savage anything that's released by a band thought to be having a second bite of the cherry. I thought we'd be no exception. The knives would be out, ready to carve the album, us and our reputation to shreds. It never happened. Quite the opposite: the album got fantastic reviews everywhere. Melody Maker said, "On this album, the Buzzcocks sound like men at the height of their creative powers." Billboard called it, "A logical fourth album that could have been released in 1981. It has all the essential ingredients for legendary status." Others said things like "astonishingly fresh, bright and strong" and, most encouraging of all, "The Buzzcocks are a band with an exciting present as well as a glorious past."

The only slightly negative review came in the NME, and even that wasn't all bad. They wrote: "Trade Test Transmissions is a grimy follow-up to A Different Kind Of Tension."

It was all positive stuff and empowered us to take on our most punishing tour yet, one-hundred-and-twenty-odd dates in twelve countries over the next eight months. That didn't include radio sessions, TV or public appearances. At one point during the tour, we flew from Holland to London in order to play at the launch party for the BBC book In Session Tonight, did a short set for The Lunchtime Show and recorded a session for The Johnny Walker Show all in one day. We then flew back to Holland in time to play a gig that night.

By the time we returned to the States, the new songs were sounding as familiar as the old ones. We were as tight as two coats of paint. The only downer of the tour up until that point was when I was hospitalised in Germany (since reported as happening in Los Angeles but, in actual fact, somewhere in Germany) after receiving a massive electric shock on stage.

As part of our stage set-up to promote Trade Test Transmission, we had these banks of old TV sets lined up and switched on at the back of the stage. Each one played a specially recorded videotape of random images. We must have bought thousands of them over the months because every night we would smash them to bits. It was our roadies' nightmare job to find TV sets in every town we visited – just so we could smash them up. On this particular night, we were playing somewhere unpronounceable and it was coming up to the smashing part. I had a special mike stand with a round hollow bottom and a hollow tubular stem, like the ones Elvis had in all those old photos. Or so I thought!

I'd developed quite a good technique of swinging it around and hitting the TV screens at just the right angle to smash them without connecting with any of the sets' components. However, that particular night someone had replaced my stand with a different one, a solid one, a perfect fucking conductor! As soon as I picked it up, I realised the difference but it was already too late. I was in mid-flight. Next thing I remember was the feeling of something hitting me in the chest with the strength of a wrecking ball. I was sent flying through the air and crashed in a crumpled smouldering heap centre stage. I was out of it and rushed to hospital, suffering from electric shock and minor burns.

People think it happened in America because Kurt Cobain said in a few magazines that he loved the Buzzers and that he'd seen one of our gigs on that tour – a gig in Boston, as it happens. He'd also said he loved the TV smashing bit so everybody assumed he must have seen us in LA or someplace. He did come to a couple of shows in Los Angeles, one at The Palace and another at The Viper Room. The Viper Room is the bar Steve Jones used to hang out at with all the Guns 'N Roses crowd: they had a sort of bar band going with the guitar player from Duran Duran.

That was where Kurt came up to us at the bar and asked us to support Nirvana on their forthcoming American tour. We couldn't do it unfortunately because our dates coincided with theirs. He called us a few days later and asked if we could do their Japanese dates. Once again, we were tied up. In the end, all we could do was their European tour which started at the end of our own worldwide trek in January 1994.

Saying yes to Kurt meant we'd only have two weeks off at Christmas before hitting the road once again, making it a total of nine months on the road and almost a solid year away from home. Of course, we said yes: Nirvana were fucking huge after 'Smells Like Teen Spirit'! It promised to be a fucking good package, plus Kurt came across as such a really decent bloke. It was hard to say no.

What was interesting was the fact he knew all our stuff and he particularly liked "A Different Kind of Tension" and my track "Sitting Around at Home", which was where he said he got that grunge sound from - the slow distorted intro and then the speeded up frenzy that followed it, repeated over and over. I didn't think too much about until I played it again years later and realised he was right - it sounds so much like their sound it's amazing, and that was 20 years earlier!

I used the two weeks off over Christmas wisely, flying to Portugal with Judith and the baby for a much-needed break and a crash course in family relationship salvation.

Christmas over and relationship unconvincingly patched up, we were straight back to it. We left the freezing cold and greyness of England and jetted off to the sun and our first dates with Nirvana in Europe. I think the first was in Madrid.

On the very first day, Kurt treated me to some of the best coke I'd ever come across. We were in Nirvana's tour bus, a big double-decker job, when Kurt brought out his stash. He must have chopped up about a gram into six lines on a little coffee table at the back. I was sitting with all three of them: the drummer Dave and the bass player with the unpronounceable surname. Kurt disappears upstairs and leaves us to it. I asked them if they wanted to go first. To my surprise, they both declined. Naturally I helped myself.

We carried on talking and drinking for a while. Before I knew it, I'd done the lot right in front of them. Just then Kurt reappeared and, looking down at the table, asked, "Where's the coke, man?" I was so busy tucking in I'd forgotten all about him.

He was alright about it: he had a never-ending supply. I never saw the other two touch it but Kurt was mad for it, so I became his tour buddy. He didn't appear to be the uptight character he was made out to be. I thought he was quite laid back: he was playing Steely Dan CDs – which surprised me. I never thought he'd be into them, but he was always pointing out little bits of their songs to me. "The finer points of Steely Dan," he would say. The other thing he was into was the artist Damien Hirst: he loved that dead sheep thing he did. He was fascinated by the insides. They had an album cover that had an angel with all her insides on display, too. I don't know if that's a coincidence or if he just liked to look at guts. He had really bad stomach problems of his own, if I remember correctly. Make of that what you will! He was doubled up with it sometimes and he had a really bad posture because of it. I don't know if he had anything seriously wrong but he was certainly suffering with something.

When I wasn't on their bus doing his coke, he would travel with us. He kept on asking me how we'd managed to survive for so long. How did we keep on going? It seemed beyond his comprehension that we could still rock out as well as we did. He would watch us every night and every night we won the crowd over. These were fucking sold-out stadiums.

I spent eleven days with him and I think we became really good friends. When the tour was over, he asked us to do the British dates too. Of course, we said yes. We played the last show in Paris before all parting company and arranging to meet up again at the Brixton Academy in London. Nirvana flew to Italy and we stayed on in France. We still had a handful of European gigs to play under our own steam.

The next thing I heard was Kurt had tried to commit suicide in Rome. He had been flown home. A few days later he blew his head off with a shotgun.

It was like the Ian Curtis situation all over again: another suicide at the end of a tour. I thought back to Alan Hughes and that fateful night at the petrol station. I thought that had prepared me for sudden death, hardened me up even, but Kurt's death shocked the fuck out of me. Maybe it was the sheer violence of it. What I did know was, it seemed like it was becoming a regular occurrence. I can't remember the exact time frame, but the same thing happened with Nico.

She moved to Manchester in the early 1990s and we got to know each other quite well. I went out for a drink with her the night before she went abroad to live. Give it a couple of days and bang! she's dead, too. I tell you that sort of thing can give you a fucking complex.

It would have been great to have played those dates with Nirvana because we had severely neglected the British side of things.

We had been away for so long we were in danger of becoming overlooked or, worse still, forgotten. I started thinking seriously about reviving my solo career. Some of the old animosity between Pete and myself had started to reappear. I started to feel I was being compromised. In fact, everything we did around that time was starting to look compromised. The packaging and visuals started to look substandard. No one seemed bothered. Also, the power was shifting ever-so-subtly: Pete was working with Tony more, recording demos for our next single. I felt our history was being devalued: we had always been concerned with both style and content but no one was paying any attention to detail anymore. We were like workhorses just doing a job. I started thinking about leaving or at least doing something else for a while.

I wasn't happy but didn't really know what to do about it. I was too laid back. Anything for a quiet life. From that point of view, I didn't have much of an argument. We tried to redress the balance in England by slotting in a tour that took us through April and May and did a few TV and radio appearances promoting a new single, 'Libertine Angel'. We did In Bed with Me Dinner for LWT and a couple of sessions for Radio One and GLR. The tour kicked off at Glasgow's Garage and took in all the usual haunts and universities. Mike Joyce joined us on stage in Manchester and the whole thing wound up in Dublin. We also fit in a festival in France and Pete was a guest on the BBC radio programme Antique Records Roadshow.

With that little lot out of the way, we went Down Under once more, did another tour of Oz and Japan. That's pretty much how it went on throughout the mid-1990s. There were highlights, like the Madstock Festival in London's Finsbury Park and a thirty-minute documentary made by Granada TV called 'With The Buzzcocks'. That was really good: we were labelled "The Punk Beatles", which I thought was cool. They showed footage of our first-ever gig filmed in silent 8mm film at Manchester's Lesser Free Trade Hall. I also played my first solo show since the Buzzers reformed. I played a one-off gig at a place called The Jackson Lane Community Centre in London with a band I'd put a band together from some musicians I'd recently met in London.

That's where I was living now.

What had happened was this: Judith and me had finally split up. I was spending too much time away. It was only a matter of time before it became obvious we couldn't carry on a relationship like that. There were other contributing factors: the fact that, even when I was in the country, I was spending an increasing amount of time in London rather than Manchester.

Oh, yes: and I met someone else. That will normally do it, right?

Not that it was as cut-and-dried as that. It was a little bit more complicated. We were never married so there was no divorce to go through but it wasn't easy by any means. I'd been with Judith on and off for almost seventeen years. Her dad had always made it clear he never wanted us to get married, so we never did. I knew he felt I wasn't good enough for her. I suppose he had some good reason to think that: I'd slept with a lot of women on the road, fair play to him. I eventually met a girl in London called Natalie. At first, it was nothing serious – well, I didn't think so. Natalie saw it completely different. She got my number and started constantly ringing the house – something none of the others had done before.

It was murder. It was so fucking obvious what was going down. I couldn't avoid it: the showdown was coming and I had to get it straightened out.

I remember it clear as day. I was feeding the baby when we received that one call too many. The accusations were made and I just had to come clean. I had an old Hofner violin bass the same as McCartney, which I picked up and started plucking. It was like a nervous reaction or some sort of safety blanket. If I was behind a guitar, I could say what needed to be said and it would all get ironed out. It came out as if I was writing a fucking song: "I've been seeing this girl, another girl."

Judith was pissed off to say the least. We sat up arguing most of the night. In the morning I packed a bag and left. I didn't go far. I booked into the Britannia Hotel in Manchester and thought I'd figure it all out from there.

I stayed there for about a week, until I realised there was no going back and got the train to London. I moved in to Natalie's flat above an Italian restaurant in Kentish Town, wondering what I'd got myself into. It was a two-bedroom place, which she shared with her sister and a friend. We had one room and her sister the other while the friend made do with a futon bed set up in the living room. It was a far cry from what I'd been used to with Judith: there was no music room or walks in the wood. It was like being back at Hartley's dropout heaven. After a few weeks of that, I realized the big mistake I'd made: I'd given up my home and family for sex. And it didn't fucking last either: we were only together for about eight months before that came crashing down around my ears as well.

This time it was down to a mixture of bad luck and sabotage and, I suppose, the little matter of another girl I'd stupidly got myself tangled up with from Warrington. This one shall remain nameless because she was a real headcase: she typified exactly how far I'd descended into my own private hell at that time. She was completely off the wall and would do absolutely anything, which was great for a while but she took things to the very extreme. One night she wanted to be pissed on, for example. I was staying with her at the Warrington Hotel and we were both pretty out of it. There wasn't much (sex wise) she hadn't tried but I drew the line at that particular request. She wasn't taking no for an answer: she just waited until I needed to go to the bathroom, burst in and made good use of the fact I was in mid-flow.

It was certainly an eye-opener. I'm not here to pour scorn on anyone's sexual fetish but that one wasn't for me.

Nor was that the bad luck I mentioned. That came the next morning, when I was on the phone to Natalie. Our tour manager knocked on my door, just as I was finishing my call, so I said goodbye to her and hung up in order to open the door. The mad bird had gone by now, because we were getting ready to leave, but everybody knew she had stayed the night.

I let our tour manager in and proceeded to tell him all about the night before, not leaving out a thing. I mean I told him every graphic detail. Worst thing I could have done: it just so happened that I hadn't hung the receiver up properly. Nat heard the whole sorry lot!

Luckily, I wasn't going straight back to London so I had breathing space to think up a believable story. It would have to be good.

I never needed one in the end. Some backstabbing bastard from our touring party made sure I'd never get to use it: we were staying in Leeds a couple of days later, playing at the Roundhay Park festival. After the gig, I'd invited two girls back to my room at the hotel. When we got there, I realised I'd been spotted walking through the lobby with them. As we got to the lift, I noticed some of our crew and support band watching from the bar. I didn't think anything of it at the time and carried on up to my floor, ready to raid the mini bar. When we got there, I cut up three lines of coke, poured the entire contents of the bar into three glasses and ordered some champagne and sandwiches from room service.

The cocktail seemed to loosen the girls up sufficiently because they were soon stripped off and getting down to it. You could say they were in full swing by the time the waiter arrived carrying a big silver tray of food and an ice bucket of champagne. Unfortunately, I had forgotten to shut the door properly. After one light tap, he walked straight in. It must have looked like a heavy porn version of Confessions of A Rock Star! There he was, standing at the foot of the bed, dressed in his little hat and gloves and asking where he should put his tray while two girls writhed about naked on the bed.

And the sabotage? That came the following morning when a phone call from Natalie informed me she had heard all about it. Someone from our party had taken it upon themselves to ring her up and put her in the picture. I never found out for sure who grassed me up. I have my suspicions that the dirty deed was carried out by one of the support band. Call it an educated guess but I'm pretty sure he knows I know.

It makes no odds now but, at the time, it left me right in the shit. I couldn't go back to the flat and I certainly couldn't go home. The Buzzers were finally off the road for a little while so I had time to go house hunting again, this time for a place of my own.

That was when my brother came up trumps: he was on the move again and he'd come across two three-storey houses right next to each other in a quiet terraced street in Highgate. Both houses needed some restoring but they were huge and full of potential. Because they needed a lot of work, we got them for a reasonable price. Roland Gift, the singer from the Fine Young Cannibals, came in on the deal. He bought the two basement flats, which he knocked through into one like the Beatles' house in Help.

I moved in the few possessions I still had during the summer of 1995 and set about turning it into a home and a rehearsal space. That was the beginning of my new life in London. It was also the beginning of the so-called BritPop scene.

Because I'd been away so much, BritPop seemed to come out of nowhere. I'm sure it didn't, but it seemed like that to me. I had missed out on most of the baggy, acid house fad that turned Manchester on its head in the early 1990s.

I'd met most of the bands though, like the Stone Roses and The Happy Mondays. I met the Mondays around the time Bernard Summer was producing them. I remember Shaun Ryder kept saying "Respect" which I took as a compliment. Their drummer had one of John Maher's old Buzzers kits which I thought was really cool. The Roses were really nice, too. They rehearsed next to Flag Of Convenience and came to some Buzzers gigs, too. All those bands did. They openly acknowledged the debt they owed to the Buzzcocks – and they weren't averse to nicking the odd Buzzers riff.

We were like the godfathers of Manchester. The respect they showed us was touching.

They took over from bands like New Order, The Smiths and us. As it turned out, none of them had staying power: they either burnt themselves out or they broke up. Certainly, by the time BritPop was the big thing, groups like the Happy Mondays, the Stone Roses and all those also-rans like Flowered Up and The Inspiral Carpets were gone.

It's always the same old story: a couple of bands come along with the same haircuts and a similar sound and they get a deal. They have a few hits and, before you know it, you've got about thirty shit bands trying to look and sound the same.

The British music industry does it every time. They fall over themselves to sign the next Sex Pistols – or the next Stone Roses – and end up spending millions signing up crap.

It happened with Punk and it happened with Acid House. It'll keep on happening because they don't seem to learn a thing. Scenes come around every five or ten years. They die out because ninety per cent of it turns out to be rubbish. When they die out, everyone says there will never be another so-and-so, but of course there will. You just have to wait five years, you fucking idiot! The bands that have genuine talent survive and all the others disappear, owing a fortune.

It's the same with the clubs and record labels that come with it – look at the Hacienda and Factory Records.

I had survived all those fucking changes from Punk and New Wave, through the crap New Romantics, Acid House, Acid Jazz, even Grunge and now here I was about to start a new band at the age of forty. Everybody was telling me BritPop is the new Punk! Of course, BritPop would go exactly the same way as every other trend but, when I arrived in London, it was just starting to take off. It was actually quite an exciting place to be. It was like Year Zero all over again. Everyone thought they could start a band. I was right in the thick of it.

I fell in with a crowd that revolved around a pub in Camden town called The Good Mixer. All the new groups like Elastica and Menswear went in there or to clubs like Blow Up or Smashing. Graham Coxon was a regular face, along with the likes of Pulp and Sleeper. The parties were endless. Once again, I found the Buzzcocks were an abiding influence to yet another generation of guitar bands, which consequently made me a most welcome guest on many occasions. They were all drunk on their fat record company advances. It seemed only right that I helped myself to their champagne and drugs.

I met Noel Gallagher at one party. He was great. I think he thought I was giving him the brush-off because I was so out of it I had sunglasses on. I was really busy trying to pull some bird. God knows what I was saying to her, but I'd been talking to her for hours. Noel came along just as I was making some headway – well, I thought I was. At that point, I noticed she was getting ready to leave so I made my excuses to Noel and left with her. I heard from someone later, I think it was their biographer Paolo Hewitt, that they thought I was acting the Pop Star. I've met up since but never mentioned that night. After all, we've all had our sunglasses moment.

My life became one giant haze, as a never-ending drug-fuelled fog descended on me, making each night merge into the next. Parties went on for days. Es were just the starters, followed by the coke and the acid and finished off with the crystal meth and heroin. My substance abuse had been on a steady increase for the last fifteen years but I knew things were seriously out of control when I found myself sleeping with a kettle and a half dozen Pot Noodles at the foot of my bed. That was all I could manage. I couldn't function anymore. I would wake up, crawl to the bottom, switch the kettle on and eat the fucking noodles. That was it; I couldn't eat solids. I wasn't even using the bathroom anymore: I was pissing in one of those plastic four-litre water bottles you buy on campsites.

I knew things had reached rock bottom when I filled that fucking thing up, I can tell you. It didn't take a genius to realize I really had no option but to straighten myself out. It was either that or end up dead.

# CHAPTER TWELVE
# NEVER MIND THE BUZZCOCKS

I realized at that point in my life that I'd pretty much taken the drugs thing as far as it could go. I'd had a good run and I'd paid a hefty price: I'd lost my family, my home, and nearly my health. I was basically at the point of no return. That's when I decided to put a new band together and get back to work. My first recruit was Welsh Pete, a bass player who'd just moved to London from Wales in order to form a group. It hadn't worked out and he'd ended up working in a clothes shop down Carnaby Street. He was a mod, which was ideal because I wanted the new band to have that sharp mod image the Buzzcocks had had for a period during the late Seventies.

In my efforts to clean up my act, I had gone back to that style, wearing dogtooth jackets and desert boots. I had also bought a couple of Rickenbackers and some AC 30s. I met him when I was in his shop one day, getting a polka dot shirt. As I was leaving he ran after me and asked for my autograph.

I didn't know he was a musician until I ran into him again at a party thrown by Justin Welch and Donna Matthews who played in Elastica. By the time we left, he was in.

Next up was another Pete, "Rock Pete": he'd been the guitar player in Roger Daltrey's solo band and played on his 1980s flop The Pride You Hide. He had also been asked to join a later version of Duran Duran. I used Phil as the drummer and we played a one-off gig at the 100 Club on Oxford Street. We broke up directly after: they were all good players and they're still some of my closest friends today but, as a band, it wasn't happening. I had to hide Rock Pete behind the speakers after a few numbers because he started going into all these embarrassing rock god poses. I decided I'd trim the band down to a three-piece after that. I replaced Welsh Pete with another mod called Chris Remington. A guy called Gary Rostock completed the line up on drums. His claim to fame was he came from a band called Easterhouse who made a name for themselves supporting The Smiths.

We rehearsed in my house for a few weeks but any immediate plans were put on hold while I attended to Buzzcocks business. We were about to celebrate the fact it was twenty years since we played the first-ever Punk festival. We returned to the 100 Club and played a nostalgic and sweaty sold-out set to an ecstatic crowd that contained a lot of familiar faces.

If playing that gig wasn't reminiscent of 1976 enough, how about the one we played not long after? The gig no one thought they'd ever see: The Buzzcocks and the Sex Pistols. We were asked to be the special guests at their reunion show at Finsbury Park.

The original Pistols line up were back, a little heavier maybe but still fucking electrifying. They were calling it the "Filthy Lucre" tour. I was happy to see none of them had lost that old spark. Some of the critics were predictably scathing (the same ones clamouring for a Clash reunion no doubt) but they didn't give a toss. Their arrogance and cockiness was fantastic, totally intact. Listening to Johnny and Steve slag off one journalist after another reminded me exactly why I'd come into this punk rock thing in the first place. It also made me realise that it's bands like the Pistols and their attitude that stop us in this country from sounding like a little version of America, with bad teeth.

Steve Jones had knocked the booze on the head, which surprised me. He was now a permanent suntanned resident of Los Angeles, as was John – although he seemed to have avoided the sun altogether. Glen and Paul still had their pale north London pallor and were still one of the best rhythm sections I've ever heard. It was a great day and just like old times. The only person missing was Malcolm, although I heard from Paul that he'd been contacted. Apparently, the band had got his number and rung him up. They then gave him all the old chat about how good it felt to be back together again, and how it wasn't the same without him. They then asked him would he consider managing them one more time. Malcolm thought about it and replied yes, of course he would: that's when they all shouted down the phone, "Well, you fucking can't." Where would we be without that sort of humour?

Fuck the critics. I had a great time. We did it all again in 2002, only this time in LA alongside America's young punk finest, like Green Day. We played a blinding set despite receiving a few death threats beforehand. They followed the Sex Pistols press conference where, according to some reports, John made some inflammatory remarks about America's involvement in Afghanistan. Some thick Yank journalist thought the Pistols were the Buzzcocks and ran a story that read, "The Buzzcocks are anti-American." At least Rolling Stone magazine knew the difference. They ran a piece the following week that said: "The Buzzcocks were easily the best band of the weekend."

As I started to pull myself together, I managed to juggle my increasingly busy solo stuff around The Buzzers' not-so-busy itinerary. Our profile in the later part of the 1990s, especially in Britain, started to slacken off. To be more precise, it fizzled out. We were back on EMI, but it soon became apparent they weren't prepared to spend any money on us, even though we recorded two more albums.

The first one was All Set, recorded in Berkeley, California, which kept us out of the country once again; the second was Modern and recorded in Barnet. Those two locations and the third-rate packaging are a good indication of our fading fame and fortune during that period. Although we did mix the second one at Abbey Road, complete with Beatle dust. Not that any settled on the album because both of them were met with complete record company indifference and consequently they failed to make an impact.

Things for us in England were so dead. Pete started making plans to emigrate to Rio. He'd got himself involved with a Brazilian girl. Unbelievable as it seemed to me, he was actually making plans to marry her and move there.

Tony in the meantime had became London's busiest bass player for hire, playing with a succession of bands that ranged from Glenn Matlock to a reformed Creation. Things started to take on a familiar feel. All we needed was for Phil to leave and we'd have had almost the exact same finish as we'd had the last time.

Then a curious thing happened: a music quiz show started on TV which suddenly catapulted the name of the Buzzcocks straight back into the spotlight. That show was – and still is – that bastard son of Pop Quiz we know as Never Mind The Buzzcocks, a half-hour panel game on BBC2.

When the idea was first put to us or to Raff our manager, the BBC said it was only going to be a one-off pilot programme or special: would we object? As far as I know, Raff agreed on our behalf so long as that's all it was, a one-off. The pilot went down so well the BBC commissioned an entire series.

Now I've never been able to get to the bottom of exactly how they were allowed to go ahead with an entire series using our name and even our logo, but that's what they did. It's done so well, it's still going strong today. In fact, it's doing so well they've put out Christmas specials, videos, DVDs and even a fucking board game!

Now I'm all for someone making a go of something and I certainly don't begrudge anyone anything. But can you imagine the Rolling Stones saying, "Yes, that's fine. Take our name and our famous tongue logo, brand your programme with it and stick it on your fucking board game"? Simply wouldn't happen, not without a few million changing hands.

They obviously banked on us seeing it as some sort of compliment – which, to some extent, it is – but come on: don't we deserve a small piece of the action? We certainly deserve something for being so fucking laid back about it.

However, having said that, I must add not everybody in our camp was entirely happy about it. Some wanted to take the matter further, because, as they quite rightly pointed out, the show does trivialise the band in a lot of ways. I'm sure there are even some kids out there that think we named ourselves after the show. But, as ever, no one could agree; as usual, it got left.

Now I'm not insinuating anything and I'm not saying I think there was any back-handers received (that I'm aware of) but it does strike me as strange that we didn't have to sign some sort of waiver or something remotely legal.

They use the Buzzcocks logo which is copyright, so that's a bit off. The BBC seem to think they're above reproach. I still have to pay my licence fee, but they can use our name, for nothing. Their attitude seems to be we should be grateful for the free advertising so fuck off. It's a tough one but

I'm not going to lose any sleep over it. Especially since I don't think we'd have a leg to stand on, even if we wanted to do something about it, because Pete went on the fucking show.

Any case we could have had against them went straight out the window right there, because it looked like he condoned it.

Clever move on their part. They knew he wouldn't be able to resist it. They asked me, too, but I told them I'm not a comedian, that's not my bag, not my thing.

I actually do watch it now. I can see it for what it is: it's for stand-up comics trying to get a leg-up, or faded pop stars that've had half a hit on the way down. Mark Lamarr is good on it. He obviously knows his music. As for the poor suckers that go on the identity parade: I wonder where their dignity's gone. I watch it and think to myself, "How come I've never seen any of the Clash or the Pistols on there?" I didn't fight the punk rock wars to lose my integrity playing charades with a fat comic.

I think Pete made a big mistake by doing it. Then again, his principles are totally different to mine. He told me he was going on that show and I said I didn't think it'd do him any favours. He wouldn't listen. He wasn't even any good: his team fucking lost.

I decided there and then that, if I was going to continue in the Buzzers, I'd have to have a safety net, an escape route. I needed to do something else besides playing those same songs every night, two hundred and fifty times a year.

Don't get me wrong: I love those songs, and I'm very proud of them. It's just that I needed to do something different. I wanted to play another style of music. I was expanding as a songwriter and needed to concentrate all my efforts on that. I had all these ideas for songs that didn't fit the Buzzcocks format: they were more melodic and bluesy tunes, a million miles away from full-on punk.

I suppose I finally understood Pete's reasons for quitting the band the first time round. The only difference was I felt I could do my solo and Buzzers stuff simultaneously. I didn't see much of the band at this point. I actually started to think it was all over. I was secretly quite pleased we'd slowed down at last because it gave me the chance to plan my future and set up a record label, Three Thirty Records. It also gave me the space to finally make the album I'd been itching to do since the demise of Flag Of Convenience, my first real solo album.

I decided that, if I was to stay in the Buzzcocks, it wasn't going to be at the expense of my solo career. That was now my number one priority. I rounded up Chris Remington and Gary Rostock once more. Together we recorded Some Reality, twelve of the best songs I'd written in years. Thankfully, that wasn't just my opinion. The album received some fantastic reviews in the monthly music press like Mojo, Uncut and Record Collector, all of which gave it a thumbs-up.

Uncut called it "unmistakably British" while the others likened it to The Small Faces and The Who. I can live with with those comparisons. When I read those reviews, it made me think back to those original adverts I'd put in the Manchester Review. It made me laugh. It may have taken twenty-five years or more but at last I was playing in a band that was into The Who.

Our first live outings also went down a storm. Before I knew it, I was doing gigs up and down the country. Things were indubitably looking up,

I was relatively clean and sober, I was in a band I loved and I was seeing my son as often as I could. On top of that, I had a new girlfriend, Lila, and work had started on the house. "Life," I concluded, "is good." I should have known better. As soon as I began to think like that, it all went horribly fucking wrong.

I was feeling so good and relaxed about everything I took my first holiday in years. I took Lila to Greece for a week.

After a couple of day's lounging by the pool, we decided to do a bit of exploring and hired a scooter. It had been a long time since I rode one but I soon got the hang of it. So I thought! On the very last day, I sneaked off by myself to a rave on the beach, where I spent a few enjoyable hours drinking red wine and smoking the odd joint. Come midnight, I'd heard enough trance music to send me into one so I climbed unsteadily back on the scooter and headed for the hotel.

As I weaved my way up the dark breezy coastal road, the effects from the wine and joints began to kick in. I suddenly felt very disorientated and dizzy. Somehow, I made it around the first few sharp bends. Then I hit a dip in the road that felt like a hundred-foot drop. I held on for dear life but, in doing so, inadvertently opened the throttle. The bike roared up on its back wheel. I came tearing out of the dip and straight into a particularly tight bend where the wheels seem to slip from under me, making me wobble wildly. I finally lost control completely and only came to a halt by hitting a fucking great rock, which ejected me over the headset. That sent me flying through the darkness, and landed me in a crumpled mess by the side of the road. I lay there in shock for a minute or so and then tried to get up. I realized I couldn't put any weight on my hands because my left wrist was ballooning up. Just then two blokes who'd seen me crash from about a hundred yards behind pulled up on their scooters. They came running over and asked if I was okay. They lifted me to my feet. I said I was fine. It wasn't until I went over to the bike and tried to pick it up that the pain really kicked in.

A sharp agonising pain shot right up my arm straight to my brain, numbing me all over. All I can remember after that was saying, "Oh, now I'm not okay" and blacking out. I came to in the back of an ambulance on the way to the local hospital where I was treated for cuts and bruises and x-rayed for various suspected breakages. The worst of which was my wrist, which by now looked like a football.

Sure enough, the results were soon back. As I suspected, it was bad news. I had completely snapped it in half, tearing all the tendons in the process. They rushed me to the operating theatre and performed what can only be described as antiquated surgery. When I woke up and saw the x-rays and the sodding great cast they'd slapped on me, I instinctively knew all was not right. I must have lain there in agony for a good four hours before the so-called specialist came along and tried to explain just what it was they had done. I listened in horror as Dr Frankenstein told me in his best Pidgin English how serious the break to my wrist had been, and what methods they'd used to reset it.

This basically involved bolting a six-inch long steel plate into my wrist which was so long that it went beyond the wrist joint and up into the palm of my hand. This effectively meant any rotation movement of my hand was now impossible. My whole arm below the elbow was now fused together like a doll's arm! It was now one continuous limb with no joints. Fucking hell! Action Man had more flexibility than me! When he finished, I asked the obvious question and steeled myself for the answer. "Will I still be able to play guitar?" He replied, "Did you do a lot of it?"

Yes, the Greek diagnosis was the worst I could have received: according to him, I would never play again.

Lila flew back to London whilst I stayed on an extra day or so to sort out my insurance and a pissed-off scooter hire. Then I followed her home and went straight to hospital for a second opinion and a glimmer of hope. Unfortunately, there wasn't one. The bone merchants at the Whittington hospital in Archway said pretty much the same thing. "My guitar-playing days were definitely behind me."

They did offer me corrective surgery but they couldn't actually give me a date. That meant I ran the risk of the bone completely setting and meshing around the metal strip. In order to remove it, they would have to cut though the tendons again and re-break the wrist. There was a lot of talk about incisions, arteries and loss of feeling in my fingers, all of which didn't sound at all encouraging. The doctor drew a lot of little blue dots on my cast to indicate exactly where the scalpel would slice and envisaging all the time about how risky it all was and how they couldn't even guarantee it would work. That's when he suggested that maybe I should consider doing a different line of work.

That cheered me up no end. What was I supposed to do? I'd been in a band all my adult life; it was all I knew. I had no choice but wait for an operation and hope. That's when I slipped into the biggest depression I'd ever known. I could not believe my career could end like this, not when it was all going so well!

It made me realise once more exactly how fragile everything in this life really is. I'd made music all these years and never given a thought to how it would end. I'd never stopped to think what I'd do if I couldn't? Then, in one short second, it looked as if it wasn't an option anymore.

As I walked home from the hospital in the pissing rain, I couldn't help thinking about how long it had taken me to reach that particular point in my life.

Before the crash, I was finally totally focused on what I wanted to do. I understood exactly where I was going and how I was going to do it. Two weeks later, here I was, facing the biggest anticlimax of my life, a low profile finish, a fade out, call it what you will. It was a crap way to stop a musical journey that'd taught me so much. Okay, I'll admit that when I started off in the Buzzers I thought it would last all of six weeks. I never dreamed it would take me around the world several times. From that point of view, I tried to be positive and thankful. After all, I wasn't fucking dying or anything. That's when the idea of this book came up, sitting in a dark corner of a wine bar off Cambridge Circus two years ago. Depressed, drunk and out of work, Terry suggested that maybe it was a good time to reflect on it all, pointing out that, as the Buzzcocks were indefinitely on hold, I had a lot of time on my hands, er, hand.

Before I go any further, I must stress that this book does not represent a totally one hundred per cent accurate sequence of events. I've tried to get as close to a time line as possible, as close as my memory allows. It's not meant to be a diary or a memoir, because that's not what we set out to do. My main objective for doing this book was to broaden people's perception of the Buzzcocks. I want to put across the fact that the band are more than a one-dimensional rock-pop group.

I think most music fans know the name, not because of a TV show, but because we've managed to keep up a reasonable profile for so many years. Another reason for doing it was due to the fact that I've never felt many people (outside hardcore fans) really know our history. Over a million people have bought at least one of our numerous compilation albums, but we did much more than just make singles. Okay, not everything was great – some stuff may not even deserve to be released on disc four of a box set – but, hey, I'm proud of it all.

I also wanted this book to appeal to people who are interested in reading about the workings of any band, not just the Buzzers, the good and the bad times. From that point of view, I'm keen to point out that it's not been a vanity project either (not by any stretch of the imagination). I'm amazed it was ever completed at all because the background to the early part of this work was such a major struggle for all concerned. In a lot of ways, it's been a story in itself. During the first few months Terry and I worked on this book, I couldn't work at all. My fingers had turned black. I was in constant pain and money was tight. It got so bad that, once the cast came off, I desperately agreed to do anything that was on offer.

I still wasn't able to bend my wrist because of the steel plate but I could just about reach some limited chords if I sat down and held the neck at a ridiculous angle. One of the offers I should have never considered was playing four solo acoustic shows with three other performers (the others being Jake Burns from Stiff Little Fingers, Jean Jacques Burnel from The Stranglers and Pauline Black from The Selecter). I'm not saying I'm above playing with those guys because I'm not. It's just that the whole thing was a bad idea. It was ill-conceived. I couldn't see how Pauline Black fitted into the equation at all: solo Ska? But the money was good and I was going crazy doing nothing. I eventually bowed out and was replaced by ex-Jam bass player Bruce Foxton. Unfortunately, I didn't do it quick enough. The west end of London was awash with posters and advertisements littered the listings. The next thing I knew, the promoter was threatening me with breach of contract. Our contract with EMI expired. A decidedly dismal Christmas came and went. Rather than repeat the experience over the New Year, I decided to go up north and visit James and my parents. That was when Judith informed me she was about to get married, that the new man in her life was going to be moving in to the old homestead, effectively becoming James's stepdad. That just about topped off 2001.

Thankfully, things started to improve in the New Year. I had a successful operation to remove the plate and Pete decided he wasn't the marrying kind after all. We met up in London to discuss the surreal and lucrative offer of supporting the Sex Pistols in LA. Following a boozy night out on the town, we both decided that, so long as bizarre events like that were still coming our way, there was still a lot more the Buzzers had left to offer. I had some pretty extensive physiotherapy and played my first gig for over a year in front of forty thousand people in LA – and then several thousand more at a festival in Rio. Talk about history repeating itself!

From then on, I can happily say I haven't looked back, er, well …outside of these pages, I mean. It's now a quarter of the way through 2003 and the Buzzers are halfway through a sold out UK tour. We're promoting the best Buzzcocks album we've done in ten years and we're still finding we're an inspiration to a lot of bands out there, whether up-and-coming or established. After the UK, we go to Europe and then on to the States where we play Madison Square Garden as special guests of Pearl Jam, a group whose leader was once a spotty Buzzcock fan who blagged his way backstage one night in New York and asked if he could carry my guitar. That was many years ago, but the cycle just goes on and on.

By the way, I don't want any jokes about having a drink with him on the last night of the tour. Thank you very much.

2003: a summary to date.

I deliberately stalled when it came to this bit because it felt like I was writing some sort of obituary. That's just about the furthest thing from my mind because the Buzzcocks are still doing great business. I've got a clearer picture of my role in there, I'm enjoying it and I'm excited again. It's a lot like starting all over again. It's difficult to sum up something that's ongoing.

People always ask me do I wish the Buzzcocks had been bigger?

If push came to shove and I had to say where we are in the great musical scheme of things, I'd have to say we are seen as something of a cult band. A fucking big cult, mind you, but a cult nonetheless. We never achieved world domination, did we? For a number of reasons (none of us were careerists, for one). That's not to say there wasn't a time when we could have been absolutely massive. We were certainly heading that way:

we were on the verge of breaking into the whole stadium rock thing. But it wasn't to be. It wasn't really us, either. We'll always be remembered for the songs. Our credibility is still intact: that's a good thing, something nobody can take away. Only we can ruin our credibility. I wouldn't have wanted to be in one of those groups who make it big on the back of one album and play all the arenas and then announce we're going to take a year off. They all do it. That year turns into another, then another. When they finally do decide to reappear, nobody gives a fuck. Everybody's moved on.

They release a half-arsed album and then they're gone. Look at Simple Minds. That's why we influence bands like Pearl Jam because we stick to our principles and never sell our souls for one more hit. Okay, we never made the big bucks that some of the bands make nowadays, but it's a totally different world now. You can get to number one on sales of nine thousand and still make a fortune advertising a pair of trainers. We sold a shitload of singles but they retailed at less than a pound and gigs cost around two pound fifty. There's more money to be earned now than there ever was, but people don't have to do as much to earn it. It makes me laugh because it's all disproportionate. The parallel that springs to mind is that story Keith Richard tells about Muddy Waters painting the ceiling in Chess Studios when the Stones were in there recording one of his songs.

Every musical generation borrows something from the previous one, everyone has influences that are passed on. That's a good thing. It's like building foundations. Sometimes it takes a new generation to raise (or revive) the profile of an artist that's gone before.

Look at it this way: we now live in a world without Joey and Dee Dee Ramone, two guys who arguably influenced a whole generation. Neither of them died rich yet bands like Green Day can already retire. What's even more bizarre is the fact Frank Sinatra made about a hundred thousand albums, died and left ninety million: Robbie Williams's already got eighty million after making three! Who's the bigger influence there?

It's fucking crazy but it keeps life interesting. It's still the best job in the world.

The important thing is to keep on striving, make the best music you can and leave a good body of work you're proud of. I hope I've been an influence in some small way; that's more important than money. It's the ultimate reward a musician can get. Especially while they're still alive and still playing.

Tragically that brings me to one of the cruellest ironies so far. Just as we were nearing the end of this book we heard the dreadful news that a great personal influence in my life was dead. I'm talking about the irreplaceable Joe Strummer who died on the 22nd of December 2002 at his home in Somerset at just fifty years old. The influence all the Clash have had on me over the years is immeasurable but Joe was a big-brother figure: he wasn't vastly older than me but he seemed a lot wiser. He had such depth to his character. That made him so very human. His passion for life and his music made him an inspiration while he was alive. Now he's gone he's become a legend. God Bless you, Joe.

And there you have it. If you've got this far, I hope you found at least something of interest between these pages.

Must go: I've a tour to catch and I'm late for the plane...

# BUZZCOCKS DISCOGRAPHY
## 1976-2003

## BUZZCOCKS

### Singles

Orgasm Addict / What Ever
Happened To?
*UP36316*

Whatever Happened To?
(12" Promo single, one side only)

What Do I Get? / Oh Shit!
*UP36348*

I Don't Mind / Autonomy *UP36386*

Moving Away from The Pulsebeat
(12" Promo single, one side only)

Love you More / Noise Annoys
*UP36433*

Ever Fallen In Love? / Just Lust
*UP36455*

Promises / Lipstick
*UP36471*

Everybody's Happy Nowadays /
Why Can't I Touch It?
*UP36499*

Harmony In My Head /
Something's Gone Wrong Again
*UP36541*

You Say You Don't Love Me /
Raison D'Etre
*BP316*

Why She's a Girl from The
Chainstore / Are Everything
(Part 1)
*BP365*

Strange Thing / Airwaves Dream
(Part 2)
*BP371*

Running Free / What Do You
Know? (Part 3)
*BP392*

The Fab Four
(7" Four Track Single)
*EM104*

Alive Tonight
(7" Four Track Single)
*PPAC3*

Innocent / Who'll Help Me Forget?
/ Inside
*ESSX2025*

Do It / Trash away / All Over You
(Live)
*ESSX2031*

Libertine Angel / Roll It Over /
Excerpt From Prison Riot Hostage
*ESSX2038*

Modern / Different
*EMI521767-2*

Jerk / Don't Come Back / Oh Shit
(Live)
*DAMGOOD214*

### EPs and 12"

Spiral Scratch
*ORG1*

Parts 1-3
*IRSSP70955*
The Peel Sessions (July 1977)

The Fab Four
*CDEM104*

Alive Tonight
*PPAC3CD*

### Albums
### (Not including reissues)

Another Music In A Different
Kitchen
*UAG30159*

Love Bites
*UAG30197*

A Different Kind Of Tension
*UAG30260*

Singles Going Steady
*LBR1043*

Total Pop
*WS021*

Peel Sessions
*SFP5044*

Live At The Roxy Club April 1977
*AFCD002*

Operators Manual (Compilation)
*EMIXDEM1421*

Entertaining Friends (Live At The
Hammersmith Odeon March 1979

Lest We Forget
(Compilation Live Album,
US Tour 1979/80)
*RE158CD*

Trade Test Transmission *ESSCD195*
All Set
*EIRSCD1078*

The BBC Sessions
*EMI49777-2*

Paris Encore Du Pain (Live) *Yeaah1*

Modern / A Different Kind Of
Product
(Two CD set that includes a
Greatest Hits)
*521767-2*

Buzzcocks
*CDBRED226*

## Box Sets

Product
(Three CD Set)
*EMICDPRDT1*

Inventory
(Complete Singles Box Set)

## STEVE DIGGLE Solo and FLAG OF CONVENIENCE

### Singles, EPs and 12"

Fifty Years Of Comparative Wealth
(EP)
*BP389*

Life On The Telephone / The Other
Man's Sin
*SIR4057*

Change / Longest Life
*WEIRD1*

New House / Keep On Pushing
*MCM186*

Last Train To Safety (12"EP)
*FOC1*

Should I Ever Go Deaf (12"EP)
*MCM001*

Exiles (12"EP)
*MCM002*

Sunset / Life With The Lions /
Sunset
(As Buzzcocks FOC)
*THIN003*

Heated And Rising (Solo EP)
*330001*

## Albums

The Big Secret
(Cassette Only)
*FAN1*

Northwest Skyline
*MCM010*

War On The Wireless Set
(US Release)
*MCM020*

Here's One I Made Earlier
*AX502CD*

The Best Of Steve Diggle And The
Flag Of Convenience
*CDMGRAM74*

Some Reality
*DEL112*

## Box Set

Steve Diggle
Flag Of Convenience / Solo

## OTHER TITLES AVAILABLE FROM HELTER SKELTER:

### Coming Soon:

**Smashing Pumpkins: Tales of a Scorched Earth**
by Amy Hanson
Initially contemporaries of Nirvana, Billy Corgan's Smashing Pumpkins outgrew and outlived the grunge scene and with hugely acclaimed commercial triumphs like Siamese Dream and Mellon Collie and The Infinite Sadness. Though drugs and other problems led to the band's final demise, Corgan's recent return with Zwan is a reminder of how awesome the Pumpkins were in their prime. Seattle-based Hanson has followed the band for years and this is the first in-depth biography of their rise and fall.
ISBN 1900924684
**£12.99**

**Love: Behind The Scenes On The Pegasus Carousel**
by Michael Stuart-Ware
LOVE were one of the legendary bands of the late 60s US West Coast scene. Their masterpiece Forever Changes still regularly appears in critics' polls of top albums, while a new-line up of the band has recently toured to mass acclaim. Michael Stuart-Ware was LOVE's drummer during their heyday and shares his inside perspective on the band's recording and performing career and

tells how drugs and egos thwarted the potential of one of the great groups of the burgeoning psychedelic era.
ISBN 1-900924-59-5
**£14.00**

**A Secret Liverpool: In Search of The La's**
by MW Macefield
With timeless single 'There She Goes', Lee Mavers' La's overtook The Stone Roses and paved the way for Britpop. However, since 1991, The La's have been silent, while rumours of studio-perfectionism, madness and drug addiction have abounded. The author sets out to discover the truth behind Mavers' lost decade and eventually gains a revelatory audience with Mavers himself.
ISBN 1900924633
**£11.00**

**Suede: The Biography**
by Dave Thompson
The first biography of one of the most important British Rock Groups of the '90s who paved the way for Blur, Oasis et al. Mixing glam and post-punk influences, fronted by androgynous Bret Anderson, Suede thrust indie-rock into the charts with a string of classic singles in the process catalysing the Brit-pop revolution. Suede's first album was the then fastest selling debut of all time and they remain one of THE live draws on the UK rock circuit, retaining a fiercely loyal cult

following.
ISBN 1-900924-60-9 **£14.00**

## Everybody Dance: Chic and The Politics of Disco

by Daryl EasleaEverybody Dance puts the rise and fall of Bernard Edwards and Nile Rodgers, the emblematic disco duo behind era-defining records 'Le Freak', 'Good Times' and 'Lost In Music', at the heart of a changing landscape, taking in socio-political and cultural events such as the Civil Rights struggle, the Black Panthers and the US oil crisis. There are drugs, bankruptcy, up-tight artists, fights, and Muppets but, most importantly an in-depth appraisal of a group whose legacy remains hugely underrated.
ISBN 1-900924-56-0 **£14.00**

## Be Glad: An Incredible String Band Compendium

Edited by Adrian Whittaker
The ISB pioneered 'world music' on '60s albums like The Hangman's Beautiful Daughter - Paul McCartney's favourite album of 1967! - experimented with theatre, film and lifestyle and inspired Led Zeppelin. 'Be Glad' features interviews with all the ISB key players, as well as a wealth of background information, reminiscence, critical evaluations and arcane trivia, this is a book that will delight any reader with more than a passing interest in the ISB.
ISBN 1-900924-64-1 **£14.99**

## Waiting for The Man: The Story of Drugs and Popular Music

by Harry Shapiro
From Marijuana and Jazz, through acid-rock and speed-fuelled punk, to crack-driven rap and Ecstasy and the Dance Generation, this is the definitive history of drugs and pop. It also features in-depth portraits of music's most famous drug addicts: from Charlie Parker to Sid Vicious and from Jim Morrison to Kurt Cobain. Chosen by the BBC as one of the Top Twenty Music Books of All Time.
"Wise and witty." The Guardian
ISBN 1-900924-58-7 **£12.99**

## The Clash: Return of the Last Gang in Town

by Marcus Gray
Exhaustively researched definitive biography of the last great rock band that traces their progress from pubs and punk clubs to US stadiums and the Top Ten. This edition is further updated to cover the band's induction into the Rock 'n' Roll Hall of Fame and the tragic death of iconic frontman Joe Strummer.
"A must-have for Clash fans [and] a valuable document for anyone interested in the punk era." Billboard
"It's important you read this book." Record Collector
ISBN 1-900924-62-5 **£14.99**

## Steve Marriott: All Too Beautiful

by Paolo Hewitt and John Hellier
Marriott was the prime mover behind

60s chart-toppers The Small Faces. Longing to be treated as a serious musician he formed Humble Pie with Peter Frampton, where his blistering rock 'n' blues guitar playing soon saw him take centre stage in the US live favourites. After years in seclusion, Marriott's plans for a comeback in 1991 were tragically cut short when he died in a housefire. He continues to be a key influence for generations of musicians from Paul Weller to Oasis and Blur.
ISBN 1-900924-44-7 **£20.00**

### Currently Available from Helter Skelter:

### The Fall: A User's Guide
by Dave Thompson
Amelodic, cacophonic and magnificent, The Fall remain the most enduring and prolific of the late-'70s punk and post-punk iconoclasts. A User's Guide chronicles the historical and musical background to more than 70 different LPs (plus reissues) and as many singles. The band's history is also documented year-by-year, filling in the gaps between the record releases.
ISBN 1-900924-57-9 **£12.99**

### Pink Floyd: A Saucerful of Secrets
by Nicholas Schaffner
Long overdue reissue of the authoritative and detailed account of one of the most important and popular bands in rock history. From the psychedelic explorations of the Syd Barrett-era to 70s superstardom with Dark Side of the Moon, and on to triumph of The Wall, before internecine strife tore the group apart. Schaffner's definitive history also covers the improbable return of Pink Floyd without Roger Waters, and the hugely successful Momentary Lapse of Reason album and tour.
ISBN 1-900924-52-8 **£14.99**

### The Big Wheel
by Bruce Thomas
Thomas was bassist with Elvis Costello at the height of his success. Though names are never named, The Big Wheel paints a vivid and hilarious picture of life touring with Costello and co, sharing your life 24-7 with a moody egotistical singer, a crazed drummer and a host of hangers-on. Costello sacked Thomas on its initial publication.
"A top notch anecdotalist who can time a twist to make you laugh out loud." Q
ISBN 1-900924-53-6 **£10.99**

### Hit Men: Powerbrokers and Fast Money Inside The Music Business
by Fredric Dannen
Hit Men exposes the seamy and sleazy dealings of America's glitziest record companies: payola, corruption, drugs, Mafia involvement, and excess.

"So heavily awash with cocaine, corruption and unethical behaviour that it makes the occasional examples of chart-rigging and playlist tampering in Britain during the same period seem charmingly inept." The Guardian
ISBN 1-900924-54-4 **£14.99**

**I'm With The Band: Confessions of A Groupie**
by Pamela Des Barres
Frank and engaging memoir of affairs with Keith Moon, Noel Redding and Jim Morrison, travels with Led Zeppelin as Jimmy Page's girlfriend, and friendships with Robert Plant, Gram Parsons, and Frank Zappa.
"Miss Pamela, the most beautiful and famous of the groupies. Her memoir of her life with rock stars is funny, bittersweet, and tender-hearted." Stephen Davis, author of Hammer of The Gods
ISBN 1-900924-55-2 **£14.99**

**Psychedelic Furs: Beautiful Chaos**
by Dave Thompson
Psychedelic Furs were the ultimate post-punk band - combining the chaos and vocal rasp of the Sex Pistols with a Bowie-esque glamour. The Furs hit the big time when John Hughes wrote a movie based on their early single "Pretty in Pink". Poised to join U2 and Simple Minds in the premier league, they withdrew behind their shades, remaining a cult act, but one with a hugely devoted

following.
**£12.99**

**Bob Dylan: Like The Night (Revisited)**
by CP Lee
Fully revised and updated B-format edition of the hugely acclaimed document of Dylan's pivotal 1966 show at the Manchester Free Trade Hall where fans called him Judas for turning his back on folk music in favour of rock 'n' roll.
ISBN 1-900924-07-2 **£9.99**

**Marillion: Separated Out**
by Jon Collins
From the chart hit days of Fish and 'Kayleigh' to the Steve Hogarth incarnation, Marillion have continued to make groundbreaking rock music. Collins tells the full story, drawing on interviews with band members, associates, and the experiences of some of the band's most dedicated fans.
ISBN 1-900924-49-8 **£14.99**

**Rainbow Rising**
by Roy Davies
The full story of guitar legend Ritchie Blackmore's post-Purple progress with one of the great '70s rock bands. After quitting Deep Purple at the height of their success, Blackmore combined with Ronnie James Dio to make epic rock albums like Rising and Long Live Rock 'n' Roll before streamlining the sound and enjoying hit singles like 'Since

You've Been Gone' and 'All Night Long'. Rainbow were less celebrated than Deep Purple, but they feature much of Blackmore's finest writing and playing, and were one of the best live acts of the era. They are much missed.
ISBN 1-900924-31-5 **£14.99**

**Back to the Beach: A Brian Wilson and the Beach Boys Reader** (Revised Edition)
Edited by Kingsley Abbott
Revised and expanded edition of the Beach Boys compendium Mojo magazine deemed an "essential purchase." This collection includes all of the best articles, interviews and reviews from the Beach Boys' four decades of music, including definitive pieces by Timothy White, Nick Kent and David Leaf. New material reflects on the tragic death of Carl Wilson and documents the rejuvenated Brian's return to the boards.
"Rivetting!" **** Q
"An essential purchase." Mojo
ISBN 1-900924-46-3 **£14.00**

**Serge Gainsbourg: A Fistful of Gitanes**
by Sylvie Simmons
Rock press legend Simmons' hugely acclaimed biography of the French genius.
"I would recommend A Fistful of Gitanes [as summer reading] which is a highly entertaining biography of the French singer-songwriter and all-

round scallywag." JG Ballard
"A wonderful introduction to one of the most overlooked songwriters of the 20th century."
(Number 3, top music books of 2001) The Times
"The most intriguing music-biz biography of the year." The Independent
"Wonderful. Serge would have been so happy." Jane Birkin
ISBN 1-900924-40-4 **£9.99**

**Blues: The British Connection**
by Bob Brunning
Former Fleetwood Mac member Bob Brunning's classic account of the impact of Blues in Britain, from its beginnings as the underground music of '50s teenagers like Mick Jagger, Keith Richards and Eric Clapton, to the explosion in the '60s, right through to the vibrant scene of the present day.
'An invaluable reference book and an engaging personal memoir' - Charles Shaar Murray
ISBN 1-900924412 **£14.99**

**On The Road With Bob Dylan**
by Larry Sloman
In 1975, as Bob Dylan emerged from 8 years of seclusion, he dreamed of putting together a travelling music show that would trek across the country like a psychedelic carnival. The dream became a reality, and On The Road With Bob Dylan is the ultimate behind-the-scenes look at what happened. When Dylan and the

Rolling Thunder Revue took to the streets of America, Larry "Ratso" Sloman was with them every step of the way.
"The War and Peace of Rock and Roll." Bob Dylan
ISBN 1-900924-51-X **£12.99**

**Gram Parsons: God's Own Singer**
by Jason Walker
Brand new biography of the man who pushed The Byrds into country-rock territory on Sweethearts of The Rodeo, and quit to form the Flying Burrito Brothers. Gram lived hard, drank hard, took every drug going and somehow invented country rock, paving the way for Crosby, Stills & Nash, The Eagles and Neil Young. Parsons' second solo LP, Grievous Angel, is a haunting masterpiece of country soul. By the time it was released, he had been dead for 4 months. He was 26 years old.
"Walker has done an admirable job in taking us as close to the heart and soul of Gram Parsons as any author could."
**** Uncut book of the month
ISBN 1-900924-27-7 **£12.99**

**Ashley Hutchings:
The Guvnor and The Rise
of Folk Rock – Fairport
Convention, Steeleye Span
and the Albion Band**
by Geoff Wall and Brian Hinton
As founder of Fairport Convention and Steeleye Span, Ashley Hutchings is the pivotal figure in the history of folk rock. This book draws on

hundreds of hours of interviews with Hutchings and other folk-rock artists and paints a vivid picture of the scene that also produced Sandy Denny, Richard Thompson, Nick Drake, John Martyn and Al Stewart.
ISBN 1-900924-32-3 **£14.99**

**The Beach Boys' Pet Sounds:
The Greatest Album of the
Twentieth Century**
by Kingsley Abbott
Pet Sounds is the 1966 album that saw The Beach Boys graduate from lightweight pop like "Surfin' USA", et al, into a vehicle for the mature compositional genius of Brian Wilson. The album was hugely influential, not least on The Beatles. This the full story of the album's background, its composition and recording, its contemporary reception and its enduring legacy.
ISBN 1-900924-30-7 **£11.95**

**King Crimson: In The Court of
King Crimson**
by Sid Smith
King Crimson's 1969 masterpiece In The Court Of The Crimson King, was a huge U.S. chart hit. The band followed it with 40 further albums of consistently challenging, distinctive and innovative music. Drawing on hours of new interviews, and encouraged by Crimson supremo Robert Fripp, the author traces the band's turbulent history year by year, track by track.
ISBN 1-900924-26-9 **£14.99**

**A Journey Through America
with the Rolling Stones**
by Robert Greenfield
Featuring a new foreword by Ian
Rankin, this is the definitive account
of their legendary '72 tour.
"Filled with finely-rendered detail
... a fascinating tale of times we shall
never see again" Mojo
ISBN 1-900924-24-2 **£9.99**

**The Nice: Hang On To A Dream**
by Martyn Hanson
ISBN 1-900924-43-9 **£13.99**

**Al Stewart: Adventures of A Folk
Troubadour**
by Neville Judd
ISBN 1-900924-36-6 **£25.00**

**Marc Bolan and T Rex:
A Chronology**
by Cliff McLenahan
ISBN 1-900924-42-0 **£13.99**

**ISIS: A Bob Dylan Anthology**
Edited by Derek Barker
ISBN 1-900924-29-3 **£14.99**

**Razor Edge: Bob Dylan and
The Never-ending Tour**
by Andrew Muir
ISBN 1-900924-13-7 **£12.99**

**Calling Out Around The World:
A Motown Reader**
Edited by Kingsley Abbott
ISBN 1-900924-14-5 **£13.99**

**I've Been Everywhere:
A Johnny Cash Chronicle**
by Peter Lewry
ISBN 1-900924-22-6 **£14.99**

**Sandy Denny: No More Sad
Refrains**
by Clinton Heylin
ISBN 1-900924-35-8 **£13.99**

**Animal Tracks: The Story of
The Animals**
by Sean Egan
ISBN 1-900924-18-8 **£12.99**

**Like a Bullet of Light:
The Films of Bob Dylan**
by CP Lee
ISBN 1-900924-06-4 **£12.99**

**Rock's Wild Things: The Troggs
Files**
by Alan Clayson and J Ryan
ISBN 1-900924-19-6 **£12.99**

**Dylan's Daemon Lover**
by Clinton Heylin
ISBN 1-900924-15-3 **£12.00**

**Get Back: The Beatles' Let It Be
Disaster**
by Sulpy & Schweighardt
ISBN 1-900924-12-9 **£12.99**

**XTC: Song Stories**
by XTC and Neville Farmer
ISBN 1-900924-03-X 352pp
**£12.99**

**Born In The USA: Bruce Springsteen**
by Jim Cullen
ISBN 1-900924-05-6 **£9.99**

**Bob Dylan**
by Anthony Scaduto
ISBN 1-900924-23-4 **£10.99**

**Firefly Publishing:
An Association between
Helter Skelter and SAF**

**The Nirvana Recording Sessions**
by Rob Jovanovic
Drawing on years of research, and interviews with many who worked with the band, the author has documented details of every Nirvana recording, from early rehearsals, to the In Utero sessions. A fascinating account of the creative process of one of the great bands.
ISBN 0-946719-60-8 **£20.00**

**The Music of George Harrison:
While My Guitar Gently Weeps**
by Simon Leng
Often in Lennon and McCartney's shadow, Harrison's music can stand on its own merits. Santana biographer Leng takes a studied, track by track, look at both Harrison's contribution to The Beatles, and the solo work that started with the release in 1970 of his epic masterpiece All Things Must Pass. 'Here Comes The Sun', 'Something' - which Sinatra covered and saw as the perfect love song - 'All Things Must Pass' and 'While My Guitar Gently Weeps' are just a few of Harrison's classic songs. Originally planned as a celebration of Harrison's music, this is now sadly a commemoration.
ISBN 0-946719-50-0 **£20.00**

**The Pretty Things: Growing Old Disgracefully**
by Alan Lakey
First biography of one of rock's most influential and enduring combos. Trashed hotel rooms, infighting, rip-offs, sex, drugs and some of the most remarkable rock 'n' roll, including land mark albums like the first rock opera, SF Sorrow, and Rolling Stone's album of the year, 1970's Parachute.
"They invented everything, and were credited with nothing."
Arthur Brown, "God of Hellfire"
ISBN 0-946719-45-4 **£20.00**

**The Sensational Alex Harvey**
by John Neil Murno
Part rock band, part vaudeville, 100% commitment, the SAHB were one of the greatest live bands of the era. But behind his showman exterior, Harvey was increasingly beset by alcoholism and tragedy. He succumbed to a heart attack on the way home from a gig in 1982, but he is fondly remembered as a unique entertainer by friends, musicians and legions of fans.
ISBN 0-946719-47-0 **£20.00**

**U2: The Complete Encyclopedia**
by Mark Chatterton
ISBN 0-946719-41-1 **£14.99**

**Poison Heart: Surviving The Ramones**
by Dee Dee Ramone and Veronica Kofman
ISBN 0-946719-48-9 **£9.99**

**Minstrels In The Gallery: A History Of Jethro Tull**
by David Rees
ISBN 0-946719-22-5 **£12.99**

**DANCEMUSICSEXROMANCE: Prince - The First Decade**
by Per Nilsen
ISBN 0-946719-22-5 **£12.99**

**To Hell and Back with Catatonia**
by Brian Wright
ISBN 0-946719-36-5 **£12.99**

**Soul Sacrifice: The Santana Story**
by Simon Leng
ISBN 0-946719-29-2
**£12.99**

**Opening The Musical Box: A Genesis Chronicle**
by Alan Hewitt
ISBN 0-946719-30-6
**£12.99**

**Blowin' Free: Thirty Years Of Wishbone Ash**
by Gary Carter and Mark Chatterton
ISBN 0-946719-33-0
**£12.99**

All Helter Skelter, Firefly and SAF titles are available by
mail order from the world famous **Helter Skelter Bookshop**.

You can either phone or fax your order to Helter Skelter
on the following numbers:

Telephone: **+44 (0)20 7836 1151**
Fax: **+44 (0)20 7240 9880**

Email: **info@helterskelterbooks.com**
Website: **www.helterskelterbooks.com**

Office hours: Monday-Friday 10.00am - 7.00pm,
Saturday: 10.00am - 6.00pm, Sunday: Closed.

Postage prices per book worldwide are as follows:
UK & Channel Islands £1.50,
Europe & Eire (Air Mail) £2.95, USA, Canada (Air Mail) £7.50,
Australasia, Far East (Air Mail) £9.00,
Overseas (Surface Mail) £2.50

You can also write enclosing a cheque (payable to
Helter Skelter Publishing Limited),
International Money Order or cash by Registered Post.
Please include postage. Please DO NOT send cash.
Please DO NOT send foreign currency
or cheques drawn on an overseas bank.
Send to: **Helter Skelter Bookshop, 4 Denmark Street, London,
WC2H 8LL, United Kingdom**.

If you are in London, why not come and visit us and
browse the titles in person!